Bachmann (Ed.)

Competence-Oriented Teaching and Learning in Higher Education – Essentials

Heinz Bachmann (Ed.)

Competence-Oriented Teaching and Learning in Higher Education – Essentials

hep der bildungsverlag

der bildungsverlag
www.hep-verlag.com

Heinz Bachmann (Ed.)

Competence-Oriented Teaching and Learning in Higher Education – Essentials

ISBN Print: 978-3-0355-1237-3
ISBN E-Book: 978-3-0355-1250-2

Bibliographic information published by the Deutsche Nationalbibliothek: The Deutsche Nationalbibliothek lists this publication in the Deutsche Nationalbibliografie; detailed bibliographic data are available on the Internet at http://dnb.dnb.de.

First Edition printed in 2018

www.hep-verlag.com

Additional materials and offers for this book:
http://mehr.hep-verlag.com/essentials

Content

Preface

To collect the essentials of teaching in higher education in a short book for busy novice faculty is a challenging if not impossible task. There are no easy recipes for coping with the complexity of processes of teaching and learning. Still, we believe it is worth trying to point out the essential considerations that faculty in any subject and in any higher education context should keep in mind when they engage in teaching. If faculty manage to shift their focus away from their own "performance on stage" as a teacher to the effect their teaching has on the learning of individual students, they are on track.

For over 10 years at the Centre for Teaching and Learning in Higher Education at Zurich University of Teacher Education we have supported faculty coming from a wide variety of disciplines, mainly from Swiss universities of applied sciences, in reflecting and further developing their teaching. Although they keep telling us how unique their teaching context is, and while we are aware of the benefits of a discipline-specific approach to faculty development, we remain convinced that some of the issues affecting beginning faculty are surprisingly similar.

Various parts of the book address three essential competences necessary to further academics' teaching approaches: the planning of a course or degree programme, the practice of active learning methods and the use of formative assessment, from a theoretical but also practical point of view. With this book, we also are looking forward to sharing and discussing experiences with colleagues teaching in other countries (e.g. in the context of various international collaborations).

Ultimately, we would like to support individual faculty in understanding their teaching as research; this means, investigating their teaching by starting to formulate hypotheses and possible questions about the effects of their respective interventions. Only with an evidence-based approach, focused on what works with an individual group of students, can faculty slowly but steadily develop effective approaches to teaching that match students' needs in a particular context. In this sense, we encourage readers to make a proof of concept of what is discussed in this book in their daily teaching practice and further develop their own strategies.

With best wishes for rewarding and effective learning processes for both you and your students.

Franziska Zellweger

Head of the Centre for Teaching and Learning at Zurich University of Teacher Education

Heinz Bachmann

Introduction and structure of the book

Essentials for teachers in higher education

It is a reality that academics in higher education are, apart from their teaching commitments, often active researchers. Additionally, many of them also work part-time in companies. Switching between these various roles has obvious advantages but often limits how much time academics can afford to spend on their teaching obligations. The situation is aggravated by the fact that traditional ways of teaching are being challenged today by the professional competences needed in the rapidly changing world of work. This publication takes these circumstances into account, at the same time offering orientation and guidance appropriate for contemporary higher education teaching and learning. The idea is not to present a comprehensive book with detailed guidelines for all kinds of teaching situations, but rather to offer a selection of topics that are considered the bare minimum for effective teaching and learning.

The following question captures the central idea of this book: what do novices who are experts in their professional field need in order to survive their first years of teaching in higher education? Reality shows that their focus of attention is often on technical expertise. They strive to become experts in their field of study and engage in research. Hopefully, during their career in higher education, they will place more and more emphasis on teaching.

This book makes an innovative contribution by consistently focusing on the essentials of teaching and learning and providing the best possible concrete and practical guidance for novices from different subject areas. **The teaching strategies presented are designed to optimise student learning**. The book attempts to address faculty's repeated pleas for concrete tips and guidance, independent of a specific country or a specific higher education institution. This publication should be useful in higher education teacher training and is especially designed to assist newly-appointed faculty to acquire the necessary skills and knowledge by themselves.

The curriculum for a Certificate of Advanced Studies in Higher Education Teaching in Switzerland serves as this book's point of departure. More than 500 academics from various disciplines have already been trained through this programme, including medical doctors, physiotherapists, lawyers, pedagogical specialists, environmental engineers, art college faculty, linguists and mathematicians. Their feedback confirmed the need for practice-related and science-based approaches and thereby helped to narrow down the scope of the book.

Tertiary-level teaching implies reflecting on what students should be capable of doing and knowing upon completion of their degrees. While teachers typically start thinking about how to formulate examinations and assignments for student assessment rather late in a module, students often want to know the assessment criteria at the start. Ultimately, what gets tested has a significant impact on directing both the students' attention and their learning behaviour during the semester. In practice, planning a learning programme is a circular process; in the end, coherence between learning outcomes, forms of assessment and teaching/learning methods is essential.

The book's structure

Our current understanding of student-centred, competence-oriented higher education means that planning a teaching unit ideally begins by focussing on how to formulate the learning outcomes. It does not consider what a teacher has to offer, but rather considers which objectives are relevant for the students. In a second step, an adequate form of assessment is selected that will allow the teacher to determine the extent to which the students have achieved the formulated learning outcomes. Questions concerning the appropriate teaching method only arise as a third step. How can one support students in their development of knowledge, attitude and skills? Here, one should particularly keep an eye on recent psychological insights that acknowledge the unique ways in which individual students learn. In fact, this book mirrors the same sequence of steps as those recommended for planning a teaching unit.

The first chapter introduces current approaches to teaching and learning in higher education. It also describes the rationale and provides a framework for the topics that follow. The second chapter deals with defining learning outcomes for competence-oriented education. The third chapter highlights the importance of reducing the complexity and amount of content to be covered, both of which are closely linked to how the learning outcomes have been formulated. The fourth chapter describes forms of assessment and their implications for course design. The fifth and final chapter deals with the design of learning arrangements that will foster the much-debated shift from teaching to learning. In a knowledge-based society, lifelong learning is imperative. Consequently, competences such as self-directed and co-operative learning need to be incorporated into the teaching and learning process.

A focus on student learning

A focus on student learning requires higher education teachers to have a basic understanding of the relevant learning theories. Each academic thereby becomes both a disciplinary expert and a learning expert. The more these teachers have to deal with teaching innovations and the pressure to use new media, the more important these insights become. In fact, high expectations that new media will bring about fundamental changes to student learning are almost sure to lead to disappointment. Despite the World Wide Web, e-learning, learning apps, software programs, MOOCs (massive open online courses), etc., the human brain, i.e. our hardware for thinking and memorising, has hardly changed on a multi-millennial time scale. Learning still happens via synapses in the brain and manifests itself in the brain's biology. German neurobiologist Manfred Spitzer used the image of a winter landscape to explain these mental processes. A person who walks through snow leaves a trail. This trail has to be used frequently to prevent it disappearing after further snowfall. The same applies to learning. To maintain traces in the memory, one has to anchor the content by regularly using it. This is the only way to ensure that it does not disappear as new information is added.

Contrary to common opinion, the bottleneck to learning is the human memory system rather than the method of presentation. Learning means taking time to practice, relating different kinds of content to one another and then integrating and applying it to specific problems. This can be done more or less intelligently, but the limiting factors – time, the amount of learning material and its complexity – remain. The capacity of humans to absorb and process information has not significantly changed over thousands of years. Therefore, reduction of content remains a core challenge for teachers: what is worth learning and how long will it remain relevant? What can, and should, be left out? Above all, one must accept that, in some circumstances, what has been learned needs to be forgotten, so that one does not continue to use old routines instead of finding new ways. Everyone knows the problem when dealing with up-dated software: we habitually carry on with the same mouse movement although the relevant button has moved from left to right. In the context of constant innovation, the force of habit often makes us fail miserably.

> *We are drowning in information, yet starving for knowledge.*
> *(Rutherford, D. Rogers, library board of directors, Yale, 1985)*

Only neuroenhancers, genetically modified humans or implanted computer chips could fundamentally change human learning patterns. Whether this is desirable, technically feasible or even inevitable is not a subject of the present or the immediate future in higher education.

This publication is the result of the editor's conviction that an academic who is equipped with the necessary awareness, knowledge and skills can – with reasonable effort – successfully deal with the challenges in higher education teaching today.

Heinz Bachmann

1 Higher education teaching redefined – the shift from teaching to learning

The following chapter gives a brief overview of current developments in society and at higher education institutions, with a view to their relevance in everyday teaching. The information presented explains the recent emergence of concepts like competences, standards, self-regulated learning, employability and the shift from teaching to learning in higher education.

1.1 Higher education teaching in view of the Bologna Process

The social significance of higher education has changed radically over the last few decades. Formerly elite institutions, accessible to only a few, have now become training centres for many. The opening up of higher education and increased mobility in a globalised world, have resulted in a marked increase in the heterogeneity of the student body. Changes in the workplace have resulted in an increasing demand for people with tertiary qualifications. Knowledge-intensive activities are replacing traditional

WAYS OF THINKING • creativity and innovation • critical thinking, problem-solving, decision-making • learning to learn/metacognition	TOOLS FOR WORKING • information literacy • information and communication technology (ICT) literacy
WAYS OF WORKING • communication • collaboration (teamwork)	WAYS OF LIVING IN THE WORLD • citizenship – local/global • life and career • personal and social responsibility (including cultural awareness and competence)

Figure 1 Framework for 21st century skills (according to Care et al.).

industries and thus also changing job requirements. Under the heading "21st century skills", attempts have been made to specify the competences needed in this new world (OECD 2018, Care et al. 2018, see also Figure 1).

The Bologna Process has to be understood in this context. What gave rise to the Bologna Process was an ambitious vision to turn Europe into the most competitive, dynamic and science-based economic area in the world. To transform such a vision into action, the Bologna Declaration for pan-European degree reforms was signed in 1999. Since then, almost 50 European countries have joined this reform process. The cornerstones of the Bologna Process are:

- the restructuring of degree courses (Bachelor/Master/Doctorate),
- transparency, compatibility and mutual recognition of course credits across all European countries (ECTS – European Credit Transfer System, workload, competences),
- quality assurance in higher education (EQF – European Qualifications Framework / NQF – National Qualifications Framework),
- realignment of higher education to fit current and expected future developments in a globalised, knowledge-based economy (lifelong learning, employability, mobility, digitalisation).

The focus on employability and competences is not undisputed, but the growing gap between imparted knowledge in higher education and the deficiencies students show in applying it is widely acknowledged. The 2015 Bologna Process Implementation Report mentions progress with the broad implementation of degree structure harmonisation. However, it also refers to significant differences in quality between participatory higher education institutions and countries that hinder student mobility and do not recognise academic credits on an equal basis (European Commission/EACEA/Eurydice 2015).

Awareness of the Bologna Process' impact on higher education teaching with its strongly learner-centred pedagogical reorientation is still absent in many places. Many countries have anchored student-centred teaching as a guiding principle in official documents. There is a well-recognised obligation to produce documentation on learning outcomes, on teacher training for higher education faculty members and on formal student evaluation of modules (European Commission/EACEA/Eurydice 2015, p. 73f.). However, there still seems a long way to go before the official policy becomes implemented as regular practice. Traditional ideas often still dominate the reflection on how to design teaching for higher education institutions. Besides thinking about the selection of teaching material, concepts on how to support student learning are rare. Considerations on how to tackle these challenges in higher education teaching will be presented in the following chapters.

1.2 Performing – learning – teaching

In the German-speaking pedagogical tradition, the term "didactic" refers to the science of teaching and learning. The term comes from the Greek word didactos and means something like "teachable". As the etymology shows, all the basic constituents that are part of contemporary higher education teaching and learning are already captured in this word:

- the activity of teaching,
- the selection of content to be learned,
- the teaching resources, i.e. the methods and media,
- the understanding of schools and classrooms as spatial and social environments and
- learning.

In the Bologna terminology, the essence can be captured in the triad "performing – learning – teaching" (see González & Wagenaar 2003). Following this triad, contemporary higher education should start by considering "performing" and only deal with questions about "teaching" at the end (see Figure 2). This means that the formal acquisition of knowledge, skills and attitudes is not an end in itself but always stands in relation to what society and the world of work demands of the graduates. Put simply, students should be equipped to cope with life in a modern society and to participate in bringing about social progress. From what is being performed, one has to infer what students need to learn and how learning is possible. Only then, in a final step, should relevant teaching designs be considered.

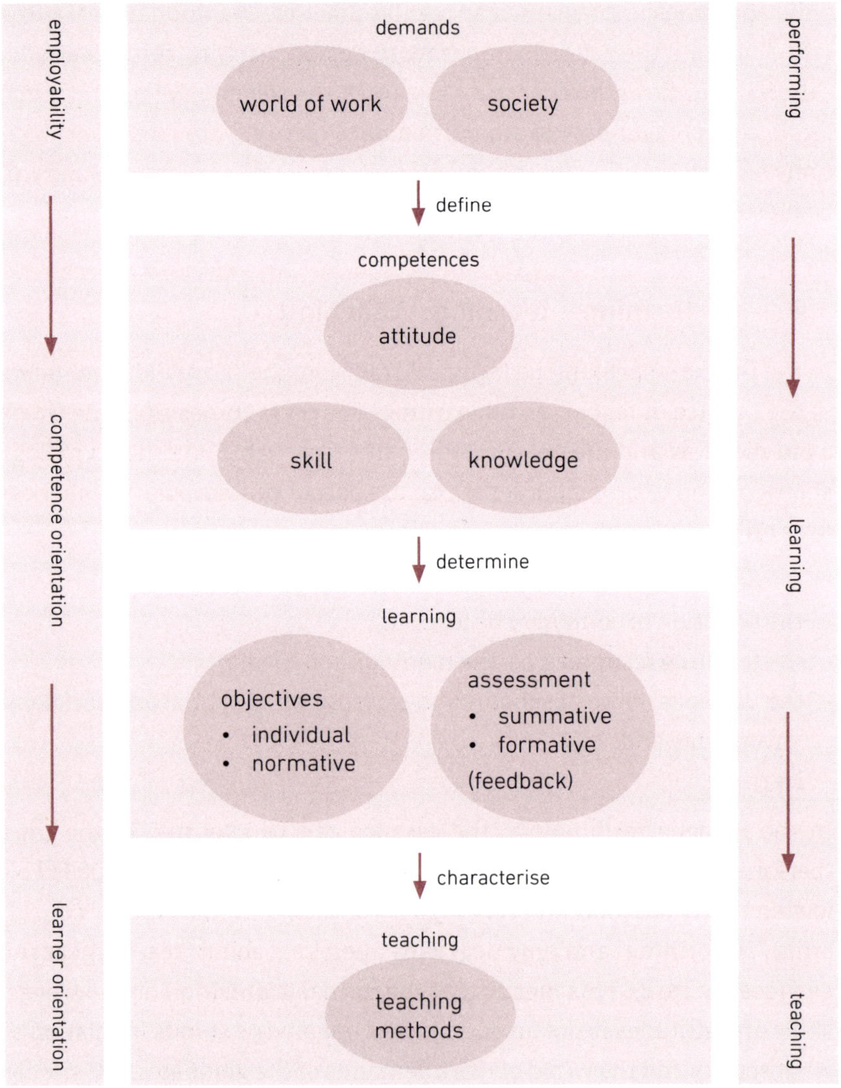

Figure 2 Relationship between social demands, learning objectives and teaching methods.

The current discussions on society's expectations regarding higher education institutions are characterised by catchwords such as digitalisation, globalisation, competition, sustainability, information overload, knowledge society and lifelong learning (see Schuetze & Wolter 2003; Rychen & Salganik 2003). One of the world's most discussed reports on this is the UNESCO Delors Report on education in the 21st century entitled "Learning: The treasure within (1996)". Although the concepts "globalisation" and "knowledge society" are controversially debated and interpreted, there is agreement that the transition from an industrial society to a globally competitive, digitised knowledge society has far-reaching consequences for the education system. In the words of Webler (2004, p. 17):

> The drastic reduction of the half-life of knowledge – except for an essential foundation of contextual and outline knowledge (orientational knowledge) – leads to the (relative) devaluation of pure factual knowledge and to the appreciation of knowledge management, i.e. the ability to develop, prioritise and structure knowledge. The worldwide problem with information is not so much the ever-increasing volume that is generated and made electronically available, but how to deal with it. This is why interdisciplinary, relatively abstract competences are becoming increasingly important. Notwithstanding criticism, this has resulted in a far-reaching consensus regarding the current development of professional requirements, described according to a list of key competences. These can be divided into four groups, namely subject-specific competences (professional expertise), self or personal competences, methodological competences and social competences. Teachers have to pass these on to their students, integrate them into their modules and revise the courses they offer accordingly.

This development away from content-centred teaching towards competence-oriented education is captured in the phrase "a shift from teaching to learning" (Webler 2004, p. 24; Kriz et al. 2014). Our new understanding of higher education practice calls for teachers to no longer focus on teaching. Rather, optimising student learning becomes the centre of attention. Learning research also supports this change in perspective (see McCown & Snowman 2014; Bransford et al. 2000; Jensen 2004; Eysenck & Keane 2015). Furthermore, neuropsychological research clearly shows that the transfer of knowledge in traditional lecture-style teaching has surprisingly limited validity (Baddeley et al. 2010).

1.3 On the way to a new teaching-learning culture

In the light of current learning theories and competences needed in the world of work in a knowledge-based society, experts generally agree that successful learning happens when (Huba & Freed 2000, p. 33):

- learning is tuned to the learners' experience and prior knowledge,
- opportunities are offered to interlink knowledge,
- knowledge is not passively transferred from one person to another, but is independently and actively acquired in a practical context,
- learners discover content and facts by themselves and reinforce it in group discussion,
- tasks demand problem-solving action plans. Problem solving and learning are driven by complex, authentic problems,
- there is enough time for independent thinking and practising. Effective learning is almost impossible under time pressure,
- self-study is prioritised and regarded as a lifelong process.

This new culture has also implications for teaching:

- teaching focuses on the active student who spends as much time as possible on independent learning (i.e. time on task) and acquires new knowledge through engaging and entering into discussion with other students,

- the teacher makes materials available and suggests methods, viewing himself/herself primarily as a moderator and coach who also structures group work as well as individual working and learning processes,
- in addition to traditional classroom teaching practices, new media is increasingly used to promote students' independent activities and to accommodate their heterogeneity.

Considering the above, it makes more sense to refer to higher education learning rather than higher education teaching. Figure 3 shows two fundamentally different positions in higher education teaching. On the left, the diagram refers to the traditional lecture format that focuses on knowledge transfer and in which the teachers themselves are at the centre of attention. On the right we see the idea of mature and independent students who set learning objectives for themselves and determine how to achieve them. Today, efforts in higher education teaching are increasingly directed towards learning arrangements that will affect a shift from left to right. Such a shift is driven by the intention to increase effective student learning and to strengthen both subject-specific and interdisciplinary competences.

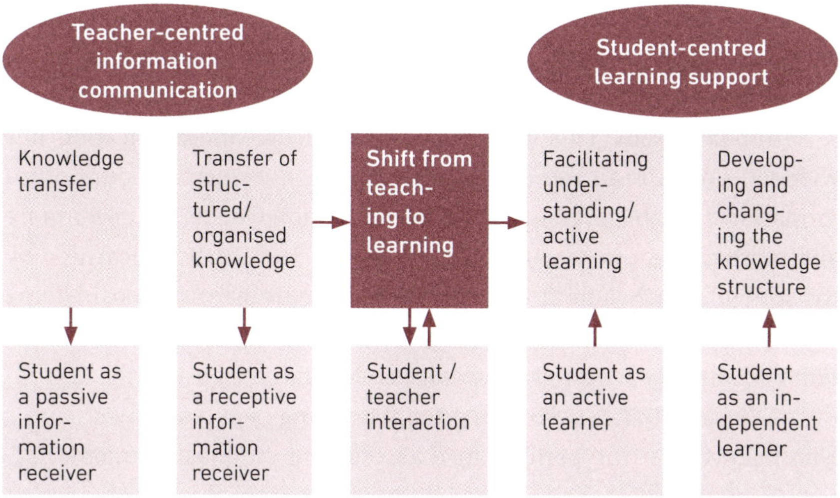

Figure 3 Teaching concepts and different roles of students and teachers (according to Rheinberg et al. 2001, p. 336).

1.4 Student-centred teaching

The different teaching concepts have implications for teachers as well as students. "Many studies have shown that teachers' concepts have a significant, and often also formative, influence on students' learning behaviour. Students adapt to their teachers' (and examiners'!) understanding of teaching and, based on their experiences, they most likely develop enduring ideas of the methods most appropriate for teaching and learning" (Rheinberg et al. 2001, p. 338).

Higher education teachers, in fact teachers in general, tend to apply the same teaching and learning behaviour in their classrooms as that with which they were socialised during their own education. Their own school success taught them what kind of behaviour helped them to progress through the education system. This is one of the reasons why it is so difficult to change teachers' behaviour. Becoming aware of these internalised behavioural patterns can be useful in establishing a new orientation. Figure 4 provides an overview of different teaching/learning activities with the corresponding, different behavioural approaches put forward by Kember and Kwan (2000).

Alexander Renkel (1994) called attention to the concept of "inert knowledge" and described his observation that students have increasingly more knowledge but are less able to apply it in practice (see also Mandl & Reinmann 2006). This gap between knowledge and application has widened since the advent of the Internet. The enormous amount of information available pressurises higher education teachers to cover more and more content in teaching, which results in superficial learning by the students. Such superficial learning boosts rote learning and, in doing so, neglects understanding, applying and connecting additional information with already-acquired knowledge and skills (deep learning). According to Viebahn (2004, p. 75), superficial learning is pursued by students who believe that the performance assessment emphasises memorisation exactly because the workload is very high. Since the introduction of the Bologna Process, students have repeatedly criticised the high workload brought on by the modularisation of courses (which entails continuous testing and assignment writing). In Chapter 4 on assessment, Feixas and Zimmermann discuss how this problem can be addressed.

Field of activity	Teaching concept – learning reference	
	Learner-oriented	Content-oriented
Motivation	Intrinsic motivation (interest, relevance of the material)	Extrinsic motivation (curriculum requirements, examination success)
Instruction	Orientation according to prior knowledge (previous experience, learning through discovery)	Material orientation (focus on material such as hand-outs and literature references)
Performance assessment	Flexible. Assessment procedure with options for the inclusion of individual interests	Frequent tests to establish learning success; the same tests for everyone
Adapting teaching to individual differences	Considering individual strengths and weaknesses	Fulfilling general performance standards without considering differences between individuals
Use of sources of experience in the classroom	Using the rich experience of the students	Using the teacher's experience and case studies

Figure 4 The activity-based classification of correspondingly different educational approaches (according to Kember & Kwan 2000).

Deep learning, in contrast to surface learning (rote learning), focuses on understanding and applying. Students who practice deep learning are those who

- rate the teaching quality highly,
- believe that they have choices regarding their learning activities,
- know exactly what a subject's learning objectives and performance requirements are (Viebahn 2004, p. 75).

The following elements are conducive to deep learning (Trigwell & Prosser 2006):

- student-oriented teaching,
- output orientation in curricula,
- content reduction in curricula.

A detailed discussion of the last two points is given in Chapter 2 (learning outcomes) and Chapter 3 (content reduction strategies) respectively.

1.5 Employability – competence orientation – learner orientation

While the previous sections emphasised the importance of student learning as a starting point for designing teaching/learning arrangements, the second central line of contemporary higher education, namely competence orientation and employability, is presented in the following sections.

1.6 Competence-oriented degree programmes

Initially, the primary aim of the Bologna Process was to align educational structures. It soon became clear that without agreement on content requirements for Bachelor and Master programmes mutual recognition of qualification levels would remain difficult.

As a result, a Qualifications Framework for the European Higher Education Area (QF-EHEA) was developed and the various countries applied this in the form of a National Qualifications Framework (NQF). Figure 5 illustrates how the competence areas (Dublin descriptors) concerning the application of knowledge and understanding differ at Bachelor and Master levels. The description is still very abstract. In comparison, the Tuning Project (González & Wagenar 2003) helped to successfully establish an agreement on more concrete, discipline-specific learning outcomes.

Competence	Bachelor	Master
Applying knowledge and understanding.	Students can apply their knowledge and understanding in a manner that indicates a professional approach to their work or vocation and have competences typically demonstrated through devising and sustaining arguments and solving problems within their field of study.	Students can apply their knowledge, understanding and problem- solving abilities in new or unfamiliar environments within broader (or multidisciplinary) contexts related to their field of study.

Figure 5 Dublin descriptors (2016) for the competence area of knowledge and understanding in Bachelor and Master degree programmes.

Degree programmes should be conceptualised on the basis of competence profiles. Reference to everyday life is central, especially at technical colleges where courses aim to prepare students for specific professions. The point of departure should be an analysis of professional requirements from various perspectives, namely those of the employers, the employees, the trainees, while also bearing educational policy in mind. Interested readers can find more details on such a vocational curriculum design process by visiting the following websites:

- http://www.dacum.org
- http://www.onetcenter.org/content.html

To end this section, an example of a competence profile developed at the Centre for Teaching and Learning in Higher Education at the University of Teacher Education, Zurich, is presented in Figure 6. The competence profile was developed together with faculty experienced in designing curricula for students and was used to create a Certificate Course (CAS) for programme directors responsible for degree programmes at universities of applied sciences; it comprises 15 ECTS points.

Area of competence	Specification
Basic academic teaching competence	You have basics skills and knowledge in higher education teaching and develop these further according to your needs.
Role competence	You understand the leadership requirements of your job and use the opportunities offered for developing degree programmes.
Competence in knowledge management regarding educational policies	You are able to analyse conceptual problems relevant to the development of a degree programme and to find and implement appropriate solutions.
Design competence	You are able to develop teaching and learning concepts for higher education purposes.
Project management competence	You can plan and calculate the resources needed for degree programmes according to basic business principles.
Evaluation competence	You can monitor the quality of degree programmes and adjust them based on student feedback and institutional requirements.
Leadership competences	You can inspire involved parties when developing a degree programme, communicate effectively and delegate work if needed.

Figure 6 Tentative competence profile for programme directors responsible for degree programmes at universities of applied sciences in Switzerland.

Such a competence profile could also be the basis for acknowledging (formally or informally) the skills acquired in the programme. However, this requires precisely stipulated standards (see Figure 7).

Standard	Level 1	Level 2
You are able to critically analyse course concepts, including the consideration of teaching and learning theories and education policies.	You can identify relevant teaching and learning theories and education policies for the analysis of course concepts.	You are able to critically analyse course concepts in a given context.

Figure 7 Standard for skill acquisition with descriptions on two levels.

This relatively simple example illustrates that developing competence profiles and relevant standards based on them is anything but a trivial exercise and one that requires considerable experience. In developing such profiles, it is often advisable to collaborate with subject specialists and dacum (= developing a curriculum) experts.

1.7 Competence – a fuzzy concept

The term "competence" refers to an ability to solve problems in concrete and specific situations. Competence orientation in higher education institutions should help students to increase their employability. The concept of competence is one that is controversially discussed and defined (Klieme et al. 2008; González & Wagenaar 2003; Rychen & Salganik 2001). Generally speaking, competences are a combination of knowledge, skills and experience that help in mastering complex situations. Competences also include motivational elements such as a willingness to solve a problem, the perseverance to overcome setbacks, tolerance in dealing with ambiguity or being optimistic that a solution can be found (see Figure 8). To cite the ECTS Users' Guide (2015, p. 67):

The European Qualifications Framework (EQF) defines competence as the ability to use knowledge, skills and personal, social and/or methodological abilities, in work or study situations and in professional and personal development. In the context of the EQF, competence is described in terms of responsibility and autonomy.

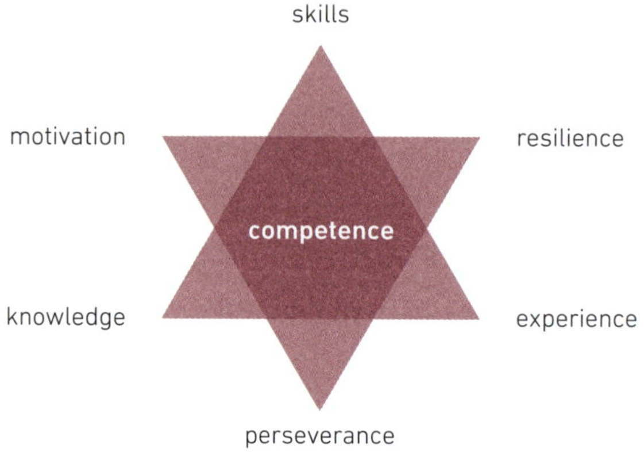

Figure 8 Elements of competences.

Knowledge-based action has become a global target in degree programmes. At the end of a programme, you will have people who can either independently or in collaboration with others find their way in unbounded, perplexing, complex and dynamic situations, at the same time solving newly encountered problems.

1.8 Key competences

The widely discussed, massive increase in the volume of information today, alongside the exponential reduction in the lifespan of specialised knowledge, is bringing about a pivotal shift in higher education teaching. In addition to conveying disciplinary knowledge, which still remains an important part of subject-specific education, practising problem-solving and developing one's own study habits have become increasingly important. As a result of the growing complexity in research and the world of work, problems must be solved in cooperation with people from other disciplines. Therefore, team competences such as communication, conflict management, resilience and self-organisation play an increasingly significant role. These key competences need to be strengthened and practised again and again; one cannot simply assume that students already possess them.

Since the introduction of competence orientation in higher education institutions, the distinction between professional expertise and key competences has become more pronounced. Professional expertise relates to the acquisition of knowledge, as has been traditionally practised in higher education institutions. In addition to professional expertise, key competences (also called interdisciplinary competences, transversal competences or soft skills) are now increasingly in demand and need to be applied in all kinds of situations. These key competences are often subdivided into methodological competences, social competences and personal competences (see Figure 9).

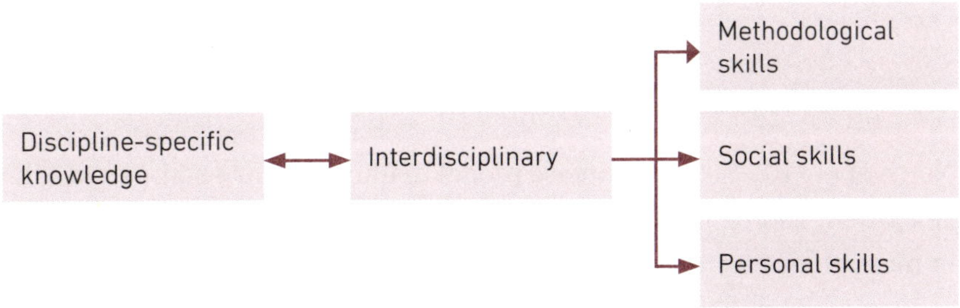

Figure 9 Distinction between professional expertise and key competences.

Methodological competences relate to knowledge, abilities and capabilities that make it possible to cope with tasks and problems by enabling the selection, planning and implementation of feasible solution strategies (Orth 1999). They include the following:

- language skills (e.g. English for academic purposes, scientific writing, presentation techniques),
- thinking skills (e.g. transfer from theory to practice, complex problem-solving),
- learning and working strategies (e.g. project management),
- information technology skills (e.g. use of specific software).

Social competences relate to knowledge, abilities and capabilities that enable us to act appropriately in our relationships with our fellow human beings (Orth 1999). They include the following:

- cooperative skills (e.g. the ability to work in a team, to adapt to separate roles in a group),
- communicative skills (e.g. dealing with heterogeneity, leadership competence),
- conflict resolution skills (e.g. dealing with bullying, resistance).

Personal competences relate to knowledge, capabilities and attitudes in which the individual's view on the world and towards work is expressed (Orth 1999). They include the following:

- self-management (e.g. stress management, self-motivation),
- ethical awareness (e.g. gender sensitivity, professional ethics),
- identity (e.g. concept of self, ability to be self-critical).

1.9 Competence development

North et al. (2012) use a staircase model to illustrate how competence development can be understood (see Figure 10). Competence development is more than just the acquisition of facts. It is important to be aware of how new knowledge is generated, i.e. by relating and connecting information to that already learned. To move from knowing something to actually doing it, practice is paramount. In addition to having the right kinds of skills, students need to be willing and motivated to implement what they have learned. One of the most challenging educational tasks is to encourage and support a change of attitude – it is even more challenging than bringing about a change in behaviour. Someone who is able to effectively analyse and solve problems in a concrete work situation is regarded as competent. If ethical standards are included in this process, we have, according to North et al. (2012), achieved the status of a professional expert.

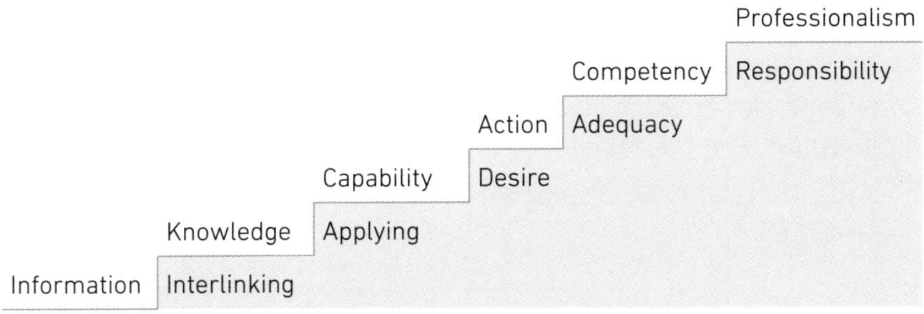

Figure 10 Competence stairway model (according to North et al. 2012).

Expert status can hardly be achieved in a regular course; to accomplish that requires a lot of practical experience. In this respect, competence transfer quickly reaches an upper limit at universities, because there is not enough time for gaining the corresponding experience. According to North et al. (2012), becoming an expert means moving from being a person who has knowledge, via being a person who can apply knowledge, to becoming a person who has all the necessary competences. Someone who has knowledge is characterised here as a person who has a little theoretical knowledge, a little practical experience, but a lack of complex problem-solving strategies. Someone who can apply knowledge knows his/her field of expertise, can organise his/her actions and can intuitively develop solution strategies. An expert has a great deal of practical experience, strong problem-solving competences and – in addition to a high level of professional expertise – convincing methodological skills. The term "standard" is often used to map this competence development. Standard refers to the expression of a particular competence according to a certain benchmark. As has already been pointed out, such standards are defined within the context of the National Qualifications Framework (NQF). It is important to note that one can only gain competence while dealing with facts. Disciplinary and interdisciplinary competences are mutually dependent. This means that in order to acquire and to teach competences, appropriate learning arrangements need to be provided, e.g. problem-based learning, case-based learning, simulation games or design thinking.

Designing competence-oriented higher education teaching arrangements means that students need opportunities to apply their knowledge. Competence-oriented higher education teaching has mostly "outcome orientation" as its focal point: which knowledge and skills, which capabilities and attitudes should students be able to demonstrate at the end of a learning unit?

This does not mean that each learning objective needs to be formulated as a competence, but together with other learning objectives it should ultimately support the acquisition of specific competences. As we can see from Figure 10, imparting knowledge is part of the teaching process, for which lecturing can be useful as one of several teaching strategies. Since competences are often highly complex, it cannot be expected that the learning outcome for each single session is a competence.

Depending on the learning outcomes, adequate teaching and learning formats have to be selected. Coherence between learning objectives, teaching/learning methods and forms of assessment is important. For example, multiple-choice tests certainly appear to be unsuitable for examining students' interdisciplinary cooperative skills. Due to new demands on students, it therefore becomes necessary to revise traditional forms of assessment (Care et al. 2018). Chapter 4 by Feixas and Zimmermann provides additional material on this topic.

1.10 New roles for teachers and students

To pave the way for competence orientation, as well as a stronger orientation to the students' learning process, it is necessary to clarify the roles of students and teachers. When an actress wants to play a certain role in a play, she has to memorise the predefined script, wear a specific costume and act according to the director's instructions. Within these contextual constraints, the actress is free to interpret and perform her role. However, if she distances herself too far from the designated role and her behaviour no longer matches the audiences' expectations, she risks becoming implausible and being rejected. Therefore, the tension between role expectations and role interpretations constantly determines role behaviour. Furthermore, the roles of the participating protagonists in a play are related and tuned to each other. Thus, for a play to take shape, the actors and actresses need to respond to each other.

With the realignment of teaching, the expectations of the roles assigned to the participating protagonists have changed. Students for example, are expected to participate more actively in class, to take on more responsibility for their learning and to build networks in learning communities. The teachers are expected, among other things, to lecture less and instead promote participative learning among the students (thus taking on roles as learning coaches). However, within this new orientation in higher education teaching and learning, expectations often remain unclear or are not well communicated, and this can give rise to misunderstandings between teachers and students.

The explanation above makes it clear that a change in role behaviour is required from teachers and students alike. It is therefore not enough to instruct only the teachers: the students also have to be prepared for the changes in study conditions. In a positive sense, learning is increasingly becoming a dialogue that can only succeed if both sides participate. In addition to continuing education for faculty, it also makes sense to communicate the changing expectations to students during introductory, first-semester lectures. An example of one successful effort in this direction takes the form of a small leaflet in which important dimensions of excellent higher education learning and teaching are presented, together with what is expected from the students on the one hand and teachers on the other (see Figure 11). By distributing the leaflet to all teaching staff and students, the contributions expected from teachers and students become transparent, thereby increasing accountability and emphasising the importance of teaching and learning. We provide a copy of this leaflet inside the book's cover so it can be used as a template for duplication.

As a student, you ...	Dimensions of excellent teaching & learning in higher education	As a teacher, you ...
... formulate your own learning outcomes. You can relate these outcomes to your own knowledge and skills. You understand the significance of pre-efined outcomes and you recognise possibilities for transfer into practice.	**Defining formulating, justifying and aligning learning objectives**	**...formulate learning outcomes that are meaningful to your students.** You find out what learners already know in order to make relevant connections between existing and new knowledge. You are an expert in your professional field and you know the key topics, concepts and processes in your subject area. You select those outcomes and contents that promote understanding and facilitate learning.
... become an active and self-directed learner. You learn autonomously and participate actively in the learning process. You make your own links between what you have to learn and what you already know. You develop effective strategies for finding, structuring and integrating information.	**Designing learning arrangements and fostering the learning process**	**... create a favourable learning environment.** You initiate and manage learning processes. You discuss the search for new information, the structuring process and the application into practice. You favour and encourage participation as well as create a challenging and supportive learning environment for your learners.
... discover new topics by yourself. You form a learning community together with other students to gain new insights and develop them further.	**Stimulating individual and group work**	**... initiate group activities.** You moderate and guide participants by proposing cooperative learning methods and problem-solving situations.

As a student, you ...	Dimensions of excellent teaching & learning in higher education	As a teacher, you ...
... engage with the content and adopt a questioning approach. You get involved in situations where problems must be solved. You allocate time for preparing and following-up on classes. You develop a critical and enquiring attitude. You take knowledge from other subject areas into account.	**Working on authentic tasks**	**... foster problem based and situated learning.** You generate authentic, complex assignments in a realistic context. You cultivate discussions in your own and neighbouring disciplines.
... ask for feedback. You use objective criticism from your teachers as an opportunity for your own personal and professional development.	**Reflecting learning processes**	**... stimulate meta cognition.** You are knowledgeable about research findings in the field of learning and teach accordingly. You show your students how to reflect on their learning.
... are able to assess your own competences and learning achievements. You are aware of your own strengths and weaknesses. You use these as a basis for improving your learning.	**Carrying out assessments**	**...assess and advise your students.** You generate outcome oriented and context based assessment tasks. You discuss results of assessments with your students and help them to identify and overcome learning obstacles.
... are aware of the degree course requirements. You comply with institutional requirements. At the same time, you make full use of the opportunities and scope which the university offers.	**Taking the institutional context into consideration**	**... take the institutional context into consideration in your teaching.** You work effectively and efficiently within the institutional requirements. At the same time, you make full use of the freedom offered by the institution to develop personally and professionally alongside your students.

Figure 11 Dimensions of excellent teaching and learning in higher education.

1.11 Summary

The current and future working environment in a knowledge-based and digital economy is characterised by:

- rapid development of technological innovations,
- rapid growth of specialised knowledge in individual disciplines,
- shortened lifespan of specialist knowledge,
- complex problems,
- global competition,
- global networks of researches, learners, consumers and industries.

In order to be successful in such a working environment, graduates need to have acquired competences to creatively and collaboratively find their way in perplexing, complex and dynamic situations and to solve problems that have not been encountered before. For the development of such competences, students need:

- professional expertise,
- skills in knowledge management,
- key competences (tasks become increasingly complex so that they can only be solved in teams, increasingly also with people from other fields and other cultures),
- willingness to learn for a lifetime, to experiment with new ideas and to forget out-dated knowledge,
- professional attitude in dealing with uncertainties and ambiguities.

This means that higher education institutions have to:

- impart a solid foundation of knowledge,
- promote network thinking (e.g. with simulation games),
- provide opportunities for cooperative learning,
- show how ill-defined problems can be solved (e.g. with problem-based learning), since it is part of everyday life and therefore part of being employable (employability),

- focus on competence orientation (alignment of learning objectives, learning arrangements and forms of assessment) instead of abstract knowledge transfer only,
- prioritise student learning,
- accept and explain that the teacher's role (in addition to being a subject specialist, also being a learning coach) and the student's role (in addition to reproducing material, also knowing how to actively solve problems) have become more demanding.

As a result of the developments described above, one can observe a shift from:

- teaching to learning,
- teaching objectives to learning objectives,
- content to competences,
- the "sage on the stage" to the "guide on the side".

1.12 Literature

Baddeley, A. & Eysenck, M.W. & Anderson, M.C. (2010). Memory. New York: Psychology Press.

Bransford, J. D., Brown, A. L. & Cocking, R. R. (ed.) (2000). How People Learn: Brain, Mind, Experience, and School. Washington D. C.: National Academy Press.

Care, E. & Griffin, P. & Wilson, M. (ed.) (2018). Assessment and Teaching of 21st Century Skills. Research and Application. Cham: Springer.

Delors, J. (ed.) (1996). Learning: The Treasure within. Paris: Unesco Publishing.

Dublin Descriptors (2016). Online (1.2.2018): http://ecahe.eu/assets/uploads/2016/01/Joint-Quality-Initiative-short-history.pdf

Online (1.2.2018): https://www.swissuniversities.ch/en/higher-education-area/qualifications-framework-nqfch-hs

ECTS Users' Guide (2015). Online (1.8.2018): http://ec.europa.eu/education/ects/users-guide/docs/ects-users-guide_en.pdf

European Commission/EACEA/Eurydice (2015). The European Higher Education Area in 2015: Bologna Process Implementation Report. Luxembourg: Publications Office of the European Union.

Eysenck, M.W. & Keane, M.T. (2015). Cognitive Psychology (seventh edition). New York: Psychology Press.

González, J. & Wagenaar, R. (2003). Quality and European Program Design in Higher Education. European Journal of Education, 38, pp. 241–251.

Huba, M. & Freed, J. (2000). Learner-centred Assessment on College Campuses. London: Ally and Bacon.

Jensen, E. (2004). Teaching with the Brain in Mind. Alexandria, VA: Association for Supervision and Curriculum Development.

Kember, D. & Kwan, K. P. (2000). Lecturers' Approaches to Teaching and Their Relationship to Conceptions of Good Teaching. Instructional Science, 28, pp. 496–490.

Kriz, W.C. & Eiselen, T. & Manahl, W. (2014). The shift from teaching to learning: Individual, collective and organizational learning through gaming

simulation. Proceedings of the 45th Conference of the International Simulation and Gaming Association, Dornbirn, Austria.
Klieme, E. & Hartig, J. & Rauch, D. (2008). The Concept of Competence in Educational Contexts. Online (1.2.2018): https://www.researchgate.net/publication/232495759_The_concept_of_competence_in_educational_contexts
Mandl, H. & Reinmann, G. (2006). Unterrichten und Lernumgebungen gestalten. In: A. Krapp & B. Weidenmann (ed.), Pädagogische Psychologie. Weinheim: Beltz, pp. 614– 658.
McCown, R.R. & Snowman, J. (2014). Psychology Applied to Teaching. Stamford: Cengage Learning, Inc.
North, K. & Reinhardt, K. & Sieber-Suter, B. (2012). Kompetenzmanagement in der Praxis. Mitarbeiterkompetenzen systematisch identifizieren, nutzen und entwickeln (2nd ed.). Wiesbaden: Gabler.
OECD (2018). Global Competency for an inclusive world. Online (1.2.2018): https://www.oecd.org/education/Global-competency-for-an-inclusive-world.pdf
Orth, H. (1999). Schlüsselqualifikationen an deutschen Hochschulen. Neuwied: Luchterhand.
Renkel, A. (1994). Träges Wissen: Die "unerklärliche" Kluft zwischen Wissen und Handeln. (Forschungsbericht Nr. 41). LMU München. Online (1.7.2017): https://epub.ub.uni-muenchen.de/149/
Rheinberg, F., Bromme, R., Minsel, B., Winteler, A. & Weidenmann, B. (2001). Die Erziehenden und Lehrenden. In: A. Krapp & B. Weidenmann (ed.), Pädagogische Psychologie. Weinheim: Beltz, pp. 269–355.
Rychen, D. S. & Salganik, L. H. (ed.), (2003). Key Competences for a Successful Life and a Well-functioning Society. Göttingen: Hogrefe & Huber.
Schuetze, H. G. & Wolter, A. (2003). Higher Education, Non-traditional Students and Lifelong Learning in Industrialized Countries. Das Hochschulwesen, Jahrgang 51, Nr. 5, pp. 183–189.
Trigwell, K. & Prosser, M. (2006). Confirmatory factor analysis of the approaches to teaching inventory. British Journal of Educational Psychology, 76, pp. 405–419.

Viebahn, P. (2004). Hochschullehrerpsychologie. Bielefeld: UniversitätsVerlag-Webler.
Webler, W. D. (2004). Lehrkompetenz – über eine komplexe Kombination aus Wissen, Ethik, Handlungsfähigkeit und Praxisentwicklung. Bielefeld: UniversitätsVerlagWebler

Heinz Bachmann

2 Formulating learning outcomes

2.1 Learning outcomes contextualised

The concept of learning outcomes is central to the Bologna Process of restructuring higher education. Learning outcomes describe what students need to know and should be able to do at the end of a degree programme. Learning outcomes have become the new benchmarks in higher education. The former orientation to input (focussing on the content that is conveyed by teachers) has been replaced by an orientation to output (focussing on the competences that students need to acquire and master).

In this book, the terms learning outcome and learning objective are used synonymously.

A key concern of the Bologna Process is the promotion of life-long learning in view of rapid economic and technological change. Formal competences acquired in schools and at universities and informal competences acquired throughout a professional career should be recognised equally. Well-formulated learning outcomes help to compare students' performances that were achieved in different contexts, as well as learners' results obtained within different education systems. The aim is to promote the career-based mobility of employees, as well as that of students. It is the only way in which it becomes evident what a student has really learned.

In this chapter, general considerations related to the concept of learning outcomes/learning objectives will be presented. Further, it will answer the following questions:

- What are learning outcomes?
- What is meant by a taxonomy of learning objectives?
- How does one formulate good learning outcomes?
- What is the connection between learning objectives, teaching/learning methods and assessment?

2.2 General considerations regarding the term objective

Objectives clearly describe a **target state** to be achieved some time in the future. Objectives specify the direction of an action. Meaningful objectives are only possible if the **actual state** is known.

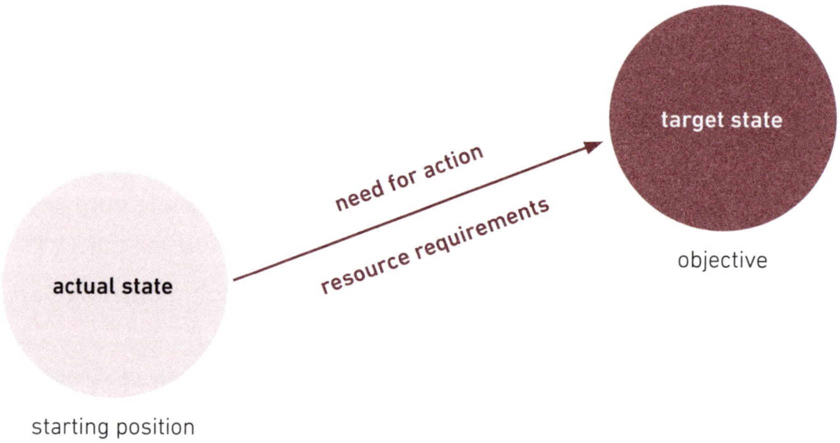

Figure 1 Good resource planning is helpful for the achievement of objectives.

The gap between the actual state and the target state determines the need for action. If the gap is too small, the target does not seem worth pursuing. If the gap is too big, the target seems unattainable and will most likely be abandoned. In order to set realistic objectives, the teachers need to have an idea of what their students already know and can do. Without such knowledge, they can easily demand either too much or too little of their students, because they will not know how many resources they need to close the gap between the actual and target states. ECTS credit points are allocated to quantify the resource requirements of the learning time needed. They give standardised information on how long an average student should take to reach a specific learning outcome.

The benchmark for acquiring one ECTS credit point is considered to be 25 to 30 working hours (workload). The purpose of the workload is for teachers to indicate how much work the students have to do for their particular subject (ECTS users' guide 2015).

The calculated workload should include time spent in the classroom, self-study time and preparation/revision time for tests and exams. One can only obtain reliable information on workload by systematically asking the students (i.e. including learner voices) and thereby gaining appropriate experience. Students' feedback shows that far too often workload information is collected arbitrarily and does not reflect reality.

To formulate clear targets, your objectives need to be smart. Smart is an acronym and stands for:

specific

measurable

attractive

realistic

time-bound.

Clearly formulated objectives help learners to:

- activate relevant existing knowledge they have,
- reduce stress, because they know what is expected of them,
- allocate limited resources (such as time),
- remain focused,
- set priorities and
- control their learning progress.

2.3 What are learning outcomes?

Learning outcomes are statements of what a learner knows, understands and is able to do on completion of a learning process. The achievement of learning outcomes has to be assessed through procedures based on clear and transparent criteria. Learning outcomes are attributed to individual educational components and to programmes as a whole. They are also used in European and national qualifications frameworks to describe the level of the individual qualification (ECTS Users' Guide 2015).

Learning outcomes state the competences students need to acquire in a module. The design of a module is therefore not based on the content to be covered during the course **(input)** but rather on what students should be able to do at the end of a module **(output)**.

Learning outcomes in the above sense are **action-oriented** and **student-centred**. Using a **verb**, they describe the expected behaviour and stipulate how this behaviour should be shown, as for example in: students can explain why the young Rilke's poems can be classified as impressionistic.

"Learning outcomes are not just an isolated tool at the level of curriculum design, (...); they are the cornerstone of the new architecture of the educational reform" (Adam 2006, p. 4). Learning outcomes, according to the Bologna Process, need to be formulated as competence-oriented objectives for each module and degree course level. To change the perspective from input to output orientation, the following questions need to be answered:

- What are the most important competences (of a disciplinary and interdisciplinary kind) that students should acquire in the module? This will then feed into the selection of the module's content.

- How can the students best acquire the desired competences? This will feed into the selection of methods to be applied.
- Which forms of assessment can be used to measure whether students have mastered the intended competences? This will feed into the selection of the most appropriate assessment methods.

Learning outcomes should be formulated as "can do statements" using active verbs (Mager 1998). The following example will again illustrate the difference between an input-oriented and an output-oriented approach to higher education:

Input orientation:

- Students are given an overview of the most important concepts concerning learning outcomes.

Output orientation:

- Students can define the concept 'learning outcome'.
- Students can develop learning outcomes for a course themselves.
- Students can present a literature overview on the topic of learning outcomes.

2.4 Learning objective taxonomies

Learning outcomes or learning objectives are often classified according to specific criteria. Frequently-used classification criteria are:

- the level of performance (e.g. enabling objectives, terminal behaviour objectives),
- the level of cognitive challenges to be met (e.g. to reproduce, to apply, to create),
- the domain of learning (e.g. cognitive, affective, psychomotor).

Education scientist Benjamin Bloom (1913-1999) developed a taxonomy to classify cognitive learning objectives (Bloom 1975; Anderson & Krathwohl 2001; Marzano & Kendall 2008). In an updated version that reflects

21st century demands, six levels of thinking skills are distinguished in ascending degrees of difficulty (see Figure 2):

- remembering,
- understanding,
- applying,
- analysing,
- evaluating,
- creating.

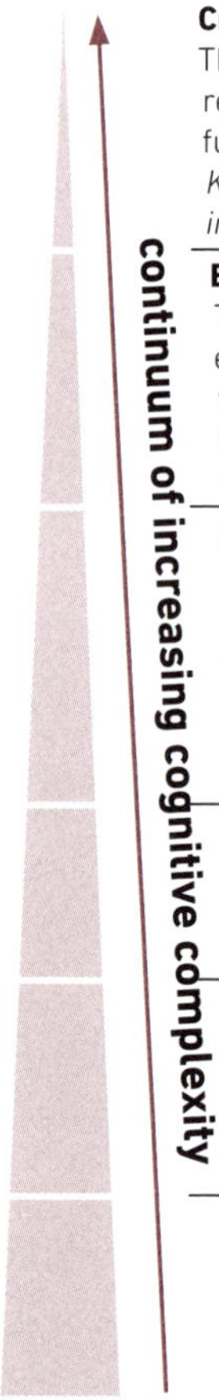

Creating
The ability to combine existing knowledge, ideas, concepts or products which require originality and creativity. This entails combining sub-sections into a functional entity by organising existing elements in a new way.
Key words: to design, to create, to generate hypotheses, to invent, to develop, to improve, to assemble.

Evaluating
The ability to make decisions and find appropriate arguments for them. This entails recognising the merit of values, assessing the quality of ideas and work based on criteria and standards. It also entails having solid subject knowledge.
Key words: to judge, to criticise, to justify, to recommend, to resolve, to reject.

Analysing
The ability to identify components, determine relationships, grasp logical and semantic structures. This entails breaking down material into constituent parts and describing how parts of a whole relate to each other concerning their purpose.
Key words: to analyse, to differentiate, to separate, to discriminate, to deduce, to induce, to appraise.

Applying
The ability to apply knowledge in problem solving. This entails transferring abstract and theoretical ideas to practical situations.
Key words: to operate, to calculate, to apply, to solve, to write, to demonstrate.

Understanding
The ability to explain. This entails constructing the meaning of spoken, written and visual information.
Key words: to explain, to paraphrase, to summarise, to compare, to contrast, to interpret, to outline, to elaborate.

Remembering
The ability to memorise information. This entails identifying and retrieving knowledge from long-term memory.
Key words: to recall, to remember, to repeat, to list, to describe, to define, to find, to select.

Figure 2 Updated Bloom's taxonomy for the cognitive domain – different levels of thinking skills.

A central concern in any subject is the ability to train students to think critically. Curiosity, questioning things, analysing facts and creatively developing innovative ideas are among the core competences required in every discipline. In the language of Bloom, this involves remembering, understanding, applying, analysing, evaluating and creating. Figure 2 illustrates the various levels of thinking we use when learning.

In lectures, thinking skills are often developed at the lowest levels of the taxonomy, namely those of memorising and understanding. Higher-order thinking is often neglected. For this reason, additional learning arrangements need to be introduced, which also stimulate the skills found in the upper levels of the taxonomy. Examples of such learning arrangements are:

- cooperative learning,
- problem-based learning,
- case-based learning,
- project work,
- flipped classroom,
- design thinking,
- research-oriented learning,
- simulation games.

These formats are easily explained, but their application is challenging for both students and teachers. They can hardly be learned and applied individually without considerable effort. Experience shows that workshops on these methods are crucial. A systematic approach is recommended to unfold the whole potential of these methods. Different teachers in different subject areas should use them to bring about a noticeable change in the teaching and learning culture of a higher education institution.

For the future, there is hope that the development of sophisticated learning software will support the teaching and assessment of 21st century skills (Care et al. 2018).

2.5 Subject-specific learning objectives

In courses with many students, it is often difficult to activate learners and do more than transmitting content. In Chapter 5 (page 119 ff.), Hanke describes how students can be activated and how to foster understanding in large groups. Another way of promoting higher-order thinking is to set specific assignments for the students. For example, team-based project work provides an opportunity for analysing practical problems and coming up with realistic solutions.

The level of difficulty for learning objectives can be defined using Bloom's updated taxonomy on the basis of two dimensions (see Figure 3). The content-related dimension focuses on the complexity of the content to be taught. This complexity needs to be assessed from the perspective of the subject area. The behavioural dimension focuses on how demanding the desired cognitive processes are. While recalling and reproducing content are not very demanding skills, application, analysis and creative problem solving definitely count as challenging cognitive processes.

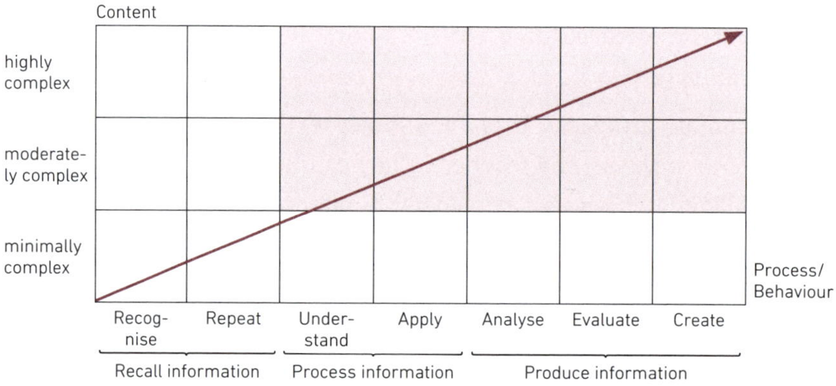

Figure 3 Level of difficulty of learning objectives (based on Bloom's updated taxonomy and complexity of content).

In Bachelor programmes, which focus mainly on acquiring knowledge and comprehending the basics, the learning objectives are often limited to recall, understanding and application. At Master's level, the focus moves to analysis, evaluation and creation. This means that interpreting information becomes increasingly important, decision-making skills should be taught and problem-solving competences, either alone or as part of a team, need to be practised. Keeping Bloom's updated taxonomy in mind helps to prevent a one-sided or narrow selection of only a few specific cognitive requirements when formulating learning objectives and in designing forms of assessment. Teachers tend to prioritise the recollection and processing of information in their classes and exams since it is much easier to assess these competences (e.g. with multiple choice tests) than to judge the production of new information (e.g. with essays or the design of a new product developed in collaboration with other students).

2.6 Transversal learning objectives (key competences)

Self-study assignments require students to be competent in skills that are widely used across different disciplines. All teachers should therefore, in addition to conveying subject knowledge, also nurture competences that foster transversal objectives (see also key competences page 28). The aim is to offer students concrete assistance and to create situations for application. Figure 4 shows a possible selection of transversal competences (key competences) that play a particularly important role in self-study assignments.

Competence areas	Examples of transversal learning objectives
Self-study competences	Students can • manage their time sensibly, • set goals and motivate themselves to learn, • deal with anxiety and stress, • organise information and recognise what is essential, • write a research paper, • present solutions they develop comprehensibly and attractively, • ...
Team competences	Students can • plan teamwork, • cooperate efficiently during teamwork, • identify and manage conflicts, • reflect on the teamwork process, • recognise their weaknesses and strengths within the team, • ...
Media skills	Students can • use media to fit the situation, • use media effectively when searching for and processing information, • find and assess information according to its quality, • consider the specifics of media communication and use different communication tools effectively and efficiently, • ...

Figure 4 Selection of transversal competences according to the self-study concept of the University of St. Gallen, Switzerland.

Promotion of transversal competences is particularly promising when they make a noticeable contribution to the achievement of a subject-specific learning objective.

2.7 Check list for formulating learning outcomes

The following points need to be considered when formulating learning outcomes:

- Focus on the outcome and not on the content to be conveyed.
- Start the learning objective with a “can do” statement.

- Describe learning objectives by using active verbs.
- Use only one active verb per objective.
- Avoid using non-specific verbs such as knowing, learning or understanding.
- Consider the various cognitive levels of learning objectives according to Bloom's updated taxonomy.
- Make sure that learning objectives are observable and measurable.

Verb lists have proven to be helpful in formulating learning objectives (see Figure 5). They present a selection of specific verbs that are suitable for each of the six levels of Bloom's taxonomy of cognitive learning objectives. Examples of specific learning outcomes are presented in Figure 6.

Students should be regularly reminded of the relevant learning objectives for them to be effective. In most cases, announcing the learning objectives only once at the beginning of the semester is not enough. It is often useful to explain the learning objectives to the students, to discuss them within the class and then to pin them up as a visible reminder. In later semesters, advanced students can also be encouraged to formulate their own learning objectives within a prescribed context. During class, teachers should repeatedly refer to the relevant learning objectives. Such repetition helps students and teachers to stay focused and draws attention to the essential aspects of the course or module.

Remem-ber	Under-stand	Apply	Analyse	Evaluate	Create
to quote	to derive	to apply	to analyse	to argue	to constitute
to state	to describe	to fill in	to select	to judge	to design
to recite	to express	to edit	to categorise	to mark	to develop
to list	to demonstrate	to use	to segregate	to assess	to construct
to label	to discuss	to calculate	to contrast	to weigh	to conceive
to name	to argue	to print	to isolate	to balance	to organise
to identify	to explain	to operate	to categorise	to classify	to prepare
to define	to explicate	to publish	to contrast	to criticise	to draft
to report	to formulate	to format	to criticise	to check	to generate
to reproduce	to clarify	to arrange	to discriminate	to estimate	to write
to recall	to present	to illustrate	to check	to appraise	to combine
to write	to transfer	to test	to differentiate	to forecast	to invent
to outline	to repeat in one's own words	to solve	to inspect	to choose	to compose
to draw	to summarise	to plan	to compare	to value	to assemble

Figure 5 Verbs for formulating learning outcomes taking Bloom's updated learning taxonomy into account.

2.8 Examples of learning outcomes

Subject	Learning outcomes	Taxonomy level
Law (University of Zurich)	Students can apply provisions for the legal capacity of natural persons to simple concrete cases.	remember, understand, apply
History (University of Zurich)	Students can: • determine differences and similarities of the Lombard and Rheinish federal government and • derive from these comparative criteria for general application.	remember, analyse, create
Biology (Open University, UK)	By the end of the course you can, with appropriate guidance: • formulate a hypothesis, • plan a suitable way of testing the hypothesis, • use appropriate laboratory equipment competently, confidently and safely, • collect data, • record data, • interpret data by placing them in the context of known theories or other information, • present findings effectively and appropriately in different formats.	create, apply, analyse, evaluate, understand
Physics (University of Hannover)	Students can evaluate different designs of thermal power-machines regarding performance and use of waste heat factors, as well as environmental and cost aspects.	Evaluate
Teacher education (Zurich University of Teacher Education)	The prospective teachers can: • formulate competence-oriented learning objectives • adequately analyse the students' learning requirements, • analyse, select and structure subject knowledge, • develop self-study assignments that align with learning objectives and assessment forms	apply, analyse, create
Health professions (Careum, Zurich)	Students can: • name the symptoms of cystic fibrosis, • describe the course of the disease, • interpret laboratory test results for cystic fibrosis.	remember, evaluate

Figure 6 Examples of learning outcomes from various subject areas at different universities.

2.9 Coherence of learning outcomes, teaching methods and forms of assessment

Teachers are challenged to align learning objectives, teaching methods and forms of assessment (Kennedy et al. 2006). In this context, Biggs and Tang (2011) used the term "constructive alignment". "Constructive" refers to the learners' efforts to understand and construct meaning through the learning activities initiated by the teachers. "Alignment" refers to the teacher's activity of designing learning arrangements that ensure that students achieve the intended learning outcomes. Additionally, teachers need to prepare appropriate forms of assessment to match these. The point of departure of any assessment should be precisely defined learning outcomes. The following Figure 7 summarises the interrelationships just described.

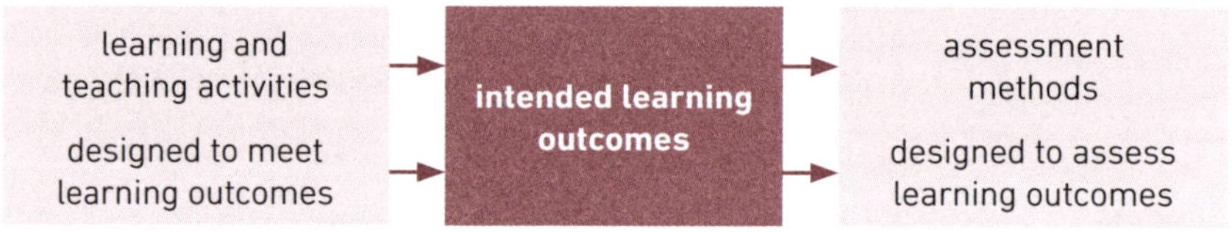

Figure 7 Coherence of learning outcomes, learning arrangements and assessment forms (Biggs and Tang 2011).

Under particular circumstances, certain teaching methods are more appropriate than others, depending on the learning objectives. Good lectures can still be relevant for conveying well-structured, factual knowledge or for promoting enthusiasm for a subject. However, in order to facilitate the transfer of new knowledge to practice, or to foster problem-solving competences, other teaching methods are more suitable (see Figure 8).

Different teaching methods	Simplified taxonomy levels according to Bloom		
	Comprehend (conveying concepts, facts)	Apply	Design, evaluate
Lecture	+++	+	+
Small group work	+	+++	+++
Self-regulated learning	+++	+++	+++
Exercises	+	+++	++
eLearning	++	+	+
Problem-based learning	++	++	+++
Exploratory learning	++	+++	+++

Figure 8 Appropriateness of teaching methods (+++ very good; + not so good) and the targeted level in Bloom's taxonomy (Exley & Dennick, 2010).

The Appendix on page 141 contains a specific example of a module description to help you plan a module that meets the above-mentioned conditions.

2.10 Summary

Learning outcomes – competence-oriented learning objectives – are the central element in the new higher education teaching structure. They are the point of reference for content selection, the choice of appropriate teaching methods and adequate forms of assessment (constructive alignment). An active verb in the formulation of a learning outcome should describe what students must know, be able to do and what attitude they should exhibit at the end of a learning process. Formulating objectives by using a suitable verb helps to focus attention on an observable learning result.

2.11 Literature

Anderson, L. W. & Krathwohl, D. R. (ed.) (2001). A Taxonomy for Learning, Teaching, and Assessing. New York: Longman.

Adam, S. (2006). Orientierung an Lernergebnissen (Learning Outcomes) – eine Einführung. In: W. Benz, J. Kohler & K. Landfried (ed.) Handbuch Qualität in Studium und Lehre. Stuttgart: Raabe, pp. 1–24.

Biggs, J. B. & Tang, C. (2011). Teaching for Quality Learning at University. Berkshire: Open University Press.

Bloom, B.S. (1975). Taxonomy of Educational Objectives, Book 1 Cognitive Domain. New York: Longman.

Care, E. & Griffin, P. & Wilson, M. (2018). Assessment and Teaching of 21st Century Skills. Cham: Springer.

ECTS Users' Guide (2015). Luxembourg: European Commission. [1.2.2018] http://ec.europa.eu/education/ects/users-guide/key-features_en.htm

Exley, K. & Dennick, R. (2010). Giving a Lecture. London: Routledge.

Kennedy, D., Hyland, A. & Ryan, N. (2006). Writing and Using Learning Outcomes: A Practical Guide. https://donstu.ru/en/Tuning%20Center/Writing%20and%20Using%20Learning.pdf [1. 2. 2018].

Mager, R. (1998). Preparing Instructional Objectives: A Critical Tool in the Development of Effective Instruction. Atlanta: Atlantic Books.

Marzano, R. J. & Kendall, J. S. (2008). Designing & Assessing Educational Objectives – Applying the New Taxonomy. Thousand Oaks, CA: Corwin Press.

Yvo Wüest & Franziska Zellweger

3 Strategies to reduce learning content

3.1 Too much content – too little time

Since the human brain's biology limits the amount of new information that can be absorbed and processed (see pages 13 and 14), reducing the content students need to learn is a core task of every teacher. This is especially a challenge for university teachers. They are experts with broad, complex, interconnected and condensed knowledge. For them it is particularly difficult – in view of what the students require or limited time budgets – to abandon or reduce content to its essence. All too often they assume that everything is important. Modules are thus often over-loaded; as a result, students lack time to intelligently process the content, which is a central prerequisite for effective learning.

In recent years, teaching methods in higher education have also changed. Competence orientation means that university teaching is less geared to transferring declarative knowledge of a subject area. Today, the focus is increasingly on developing skills that enable learners to act competently in unforeseen situations. Subsequently, new objectives and teaching formats come into focus. At the same time, teachers are increasingly confronted with students who have different learning requirements.

Ultimately, the fast growing body of new knowledge in every discipline shows that completeness is no longer possible and meaningful. It takes courage to leave gaps, and it also takes instruments and techniques to reduce content, as well as to simplify its complexity. It forces teachers to think more about the learning needs of their students. As a consequence, teachers who systematically reduce the amount and complexity of the content, improve the quality and comprehensibility of their teaching and make it easier for students to access the subject. This chapter describes how teachers can identify core concepts and reduce complexity of challenging topics corresponding to the learning needs of students. Additionally, information will be presented on how teachers can encourage students to take a "reductive" approach themselves.

3.2 Reduction – what is the teacher's task?

As soon as teachers start to select content, they can already ask themselves questions that help to narrow down that content (Lehner 2013, p. 41):

1. Which content is relevant for my target group?
2. Which learning objectives should I focus on? What should students essentially gain from the classes?
3. How much time is available for learning certain content or for developing a certain competence?

In short, the essential parameters of planning a teaching unit are the learners' characteristics, the learning objectives (see Chapter 2) and the time available. In accordance with "constructive alignment" (Biggs 2007) mentioned by Bachmann in Chapter 2, teachers try to design learning units in a way that students can achieve the intended learning outcomes in the available time. Ideally, students will succeed in constructing their personal meaning through the learning activities, choice of material, presentation and new learning experiences, thereby developing the desired competences.

Criteria presented many years ago by Wolfgang Klafki – a German researcher in pedagogy – offer an important point of reference for the selection and justification of learning content (Klafki 1958; Kron et al. 2014). The essential question is: "What value does the planned content have for the students?" Klafki distinguishes five value dimensions:

1. **Exemplary significance:** How can students use what they have learned today? To what general information or problem does the specific content relate?

2. **Contemporary significance:** What does it mean for students right now? What does the relevant content mean for the students and – from a pedagogical point of view – what meaning should it have?
3. **Future significance:** What does the content mean for the students in the future? What is the significance of the content – the topic – for the students' future?
4. **Content structure:** Which structure is most suitable for the content (placed in a certain perspective by questions 2 and 3)?
5. **Accessibility:** How can I support the students with processing the content and which tools are helpful?

These five points provide different perspectives on planning a teaching unit. The first three points explain the reason why the unit should include particular content. In a next step the content must be structured. The clarification of accessibility is thereby particularly important: which special cases, phenomena, situations and experiments can be introduced to make the respective content structures interesting, accessible, comprehensible and descriptive for students in a particular module or at a specific level of education?

Klafki (1958) went even further with his ideas. He said: "Only if the educational content has a concrete value, as well as an actual educational value, can the choice of this content be sufficiently justified."

As shown in the discussion about improved accessibility, **the challenge is not only to reduce the amount of material, but also to reduce its complexity**. This is done so that students can better absorb the material in the available time (Lehner 2012, p. 11). As a first step, Lehner advises teachers to concentrate on the essentials, i.e. on terms, structures and concepts, which are essential to the target group and their objectives. As a second step, content must be simplified so that the target group can grasp it.

The following two examples illustrate these steps of concentration and simplification.

Example 1: Teaching material for introducing natural sciences

The primary school textbook "Phänomenal" contains material that is used to introduce scientific phenomena to pupils from grade five upwards. In the chapter titled "Loud and Soft – Acoustics", the teaching material concentrates on the development of sounds and noises in order to illustrate their occurrence and distribution. The chapter concludes with a focus on protection against noise. Major importance is attached to the conceptualisation as well as to the introduction of scientific working methods.

How the auditory system functions is a core concept in the chapter about acoustics. The following illustration (see Figure 1) – accompanied by a short text – simplifies how hearing works so that children of this age group can grasp the central elements and mechanisms of hearing. The basic elements and their interaction are sufficient to further understand acoustic phenomena. The type of presentation is suitable for deepening and differentiating the concept in biology lessons later on.

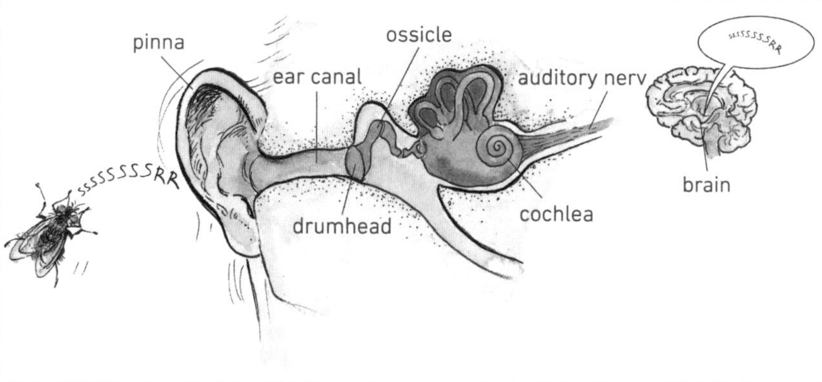

Figure 1 Our ear (Schwengeler et al. 2002, p.22).

Example 2: Guidelines for developing a Master's thesis in the context of teacher education

At the Zurich University of Teacher Education, final-year students on the 4-year programme for secondary school teaching work on a Master's thesis over a period of 8 months. They thereby demonstrate their ability to develop in-depth knowledge in a particular field and to make an original contribution to the research discourse.

The team of the writing centre developed guidelines (Ammann & Hermann 2017) to support students (and their mentors) in the process of writing a Master's thesis; writing such guidelines is a challenging reductive task, as scientific writing is complex. The result is a well-structured 30-page brochure, including key concepts of scientific writing such as developing a research question and building a strong argument, as well as checklists, e.g. on how to keep writing, on how to structure a scientific text.

The essence of scientific writing is captured in the following illustration:

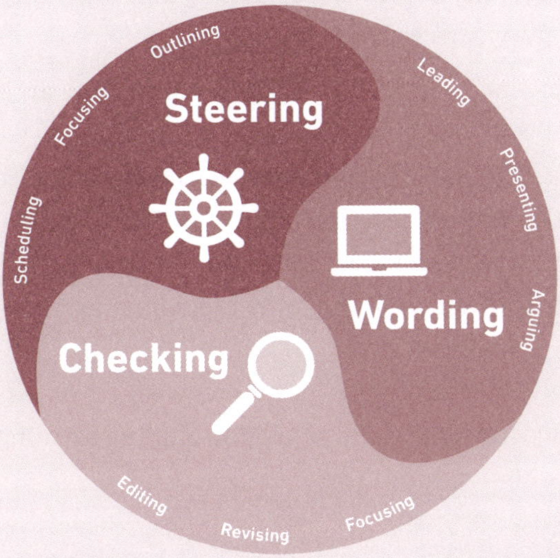

Figure 2 Triadic model of writing.

Not only do students need project-management skills to support the advancement of their project (steering), but they also need to produce an academic piece of writing, i.e. compose a well-structured text that argues convincingly and describes the scientific methods (wording). At the same time, a third mode focuses on iterative procedures of assessing and reassessing the text in progress (checking). As the illustration shows, these major activities are intertwined and include various techniques and subroutines. Like a compass, it supports students in understanding the intricacies of the writing process; it suggests a non-linear approach, encouraging them to start developing and revising text from an early stage. The authors took great care with their choice of the three keywords and the adapted pictograms to convey their key messages.

After the considerations and examples in this chapter, it becomes clear that the demand for reduction is plausible and quickly established – but the task itself should not be underestimated. The job of preparing material for teaching units becomes a balancing act, especially for university teachers. It is always necessary to rebalance:

- complete coverage of the learning content with an exemplary approach,
- the amount of detailed knowledge learners need in order to grasp higher-level concepts,
- the extent to which content can be simplified to further differentiate and deepen knowledge throughout the whole extent of the learning process,
- how strongly heterogeneous prior knowledge can be activated and taken into account while still achieving binding learning objectives for everybody.

3.3 Selection and preparation of learning content in four steps

Every planning stage, whether for an entire semester or a single lesson, requires a conscious examination of the learning content. Based on the ideas from the previous sections, we recommend a four-step procedure:

Step	Questions	Guidelines
1. Establishing and refining the topic	• Are there competences that need to be defined and developed? • Does the institution have content specifications that influence the treatment of the topic or the choice of content? • What is the topic's guiding principle? • How do students relate to the topic? • How do I, as a teacher, connect to the topic?	Information from the conceptual framework, the curriculum or the teaching assignment will help you to analyse both the contextual conditions and the participants.
2. Collecting and organising subject content	• What is the topic's inner, logical structure? • What content – from a subject-specific point of view – is absolutely essential for the topic? • How do the various content elements relate to each other and are there umbrella terms, as well as narrower terms? • What are the essential key areas and facts, thereby determining what content is needed for understanding the subject? • What is secondary – what can I omit, if necessary?	This calls for professional competence. It needs an "eye for the big picture and the details." A mind map often helps to work out core concepts and to structure them in an orderly manner. The teachers can use an Advance Organizer to give the students a preview of the course's structure, which the students can use as an overview later on. More about Advance Organizers in the next section.

Step	Questions	Guidelines
3. Selecting and weighting important learning content (with a focus on the students' learning needs)	• Which aspects of the content are particularly relevant for the students' personal or professional situation? Which aspects are less relevant (concentration)? • What is the central learning step that students should take? • What is likely to be easy for the students and where might they encounter difficulties? • How can difficult content be simplified to promote understanding?	First clarify the students' learning requirements. For a meaningful selection, use the umbrella terms from point 2 in this table. Then use the learning content to set the focal points.
4. Compare the amount of content with the available time	• How much time is available? • How is the time (roughly) distributed among the different key areas of the topic? • Can the selected learning content be processed during this time?	This involves the type of processing, i.e. the choice of teaching methods. You should always be guided by the available time.

Figure 3 Steps, questions and guidelines for the preparation of learning content.

3.4 Methods for the reduction of learning content

In the following section, some methodological guidelines are provided. They help teachers, especially in the third and fourth steps stipulated by Klafki (see page 59), to prepare and teach sophisticated learning content such that students can process it in the available time.

It should be noted, however, that this reduction process requires deep expert knowledge on the subject. One successful approach to catalysing this process could be an exchange among teachers in the same subject area. They would have to intensively discuss – even argue – to decide which concrete content and concepts are suitable for developing a topic in the long term and how students can be optimally supported in notoriously difficult learning steps. However, there are certain methodological guidelines that can help everybody. On the one hand, an "Advance

Organizer" is a method for teachers to inform and orientate the students about the subject matter, at the same time focussing on central aspects by means of "key messages". On the other hand, the students themselves should be encouraged to actively deal with reducing the subject matter on their own.

3.4.1 Advance Organizer

An Advance Organizer (AO) provides an initial orientation on the subject matter. It is a comprehensive expert's view, presented on a relatively abstract level and which shows the central interrelationships in a topic; it aims to support the students in seeing the big picture and to anchor it sustainably. This also prevents students from getting lost in detail (Mayer 1979). The teacher's intention is to mobilise the students' prior knowledge with the AO and, thus, also to facilitate their understanding.

An AO is usually introduced at the beginning of a new learning unit for about ten to fifteen minutes maximum. The teacher presents approximately ten to fifteen terms, fundamental ideas, concepts and/or questions on a slide or hard copy. By suggesting connections and visualising special phenomena, the teacher provides the students with an expert structure early (i.e. in advance) in the learning process. This makes it easier for students to build on existing knowledge and construct new knowledge independently. The AO can also be an important point of reference during or at the end of a course.

The following two examples illustrate the idea of an Advance Organizer and its practical use in the classroom:

> Example – Moderation Techniques (Seminar by Yvo Wüest for Health Professionals):
>
> The following Advance Organizer was used in a training course with teachers in the health sector. At the planning stage, two days were devoted to the topic "moderation techniques". Since only half a day

was left for this topic after a revision of the learning content, reductive considerations were necessary.

The teacher showed the basic structure with a mind map that illustrated the essential content of the topic “moderation techniques”. Three in-depth examples were selected, which represented the content that could be realistically processed in the shortened time span.

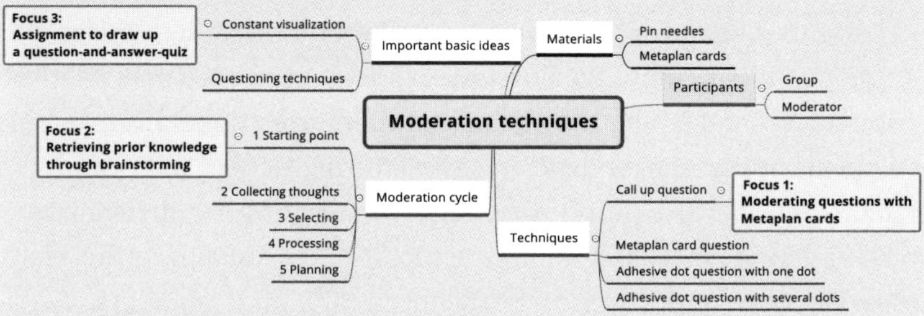

Figure 4 Mind map used as an Advance Organizer (Wüest 2017).

The experience with the Advance Organizer has been consistently positive. With such an overview, students began to recognise how the learning content is embedded in the subject area. They gained particular benefit by examining three exemplary methods with which they can switch the function of the moderation within a group, depending on the focus required at each phase.

Example – X-ray Crystallography (Lecture by Dr. Sabina Gerber)

The curriculum of the sixth semester of the Bachelor’s degree programme in chemistry includes the topic of the structural clarification of proteins using X-ray crystallography and covers various methods for the bioanalytics of proteins. The teaching format is a series of lectures with thirty to forty participants at the Zurich University of Applied Sciences (ZHAW) in Wädenswil, Switzerland. The X-ray crystallography of proteins is a highly specialised bioanalytical method, mostly used in an academic environment. Students who attended this course had prior scientific knowledge from various apprenticeships, mainly in the fields of chemistry and biology. However, most of them had no prior knowledge about X-ray crystallography.

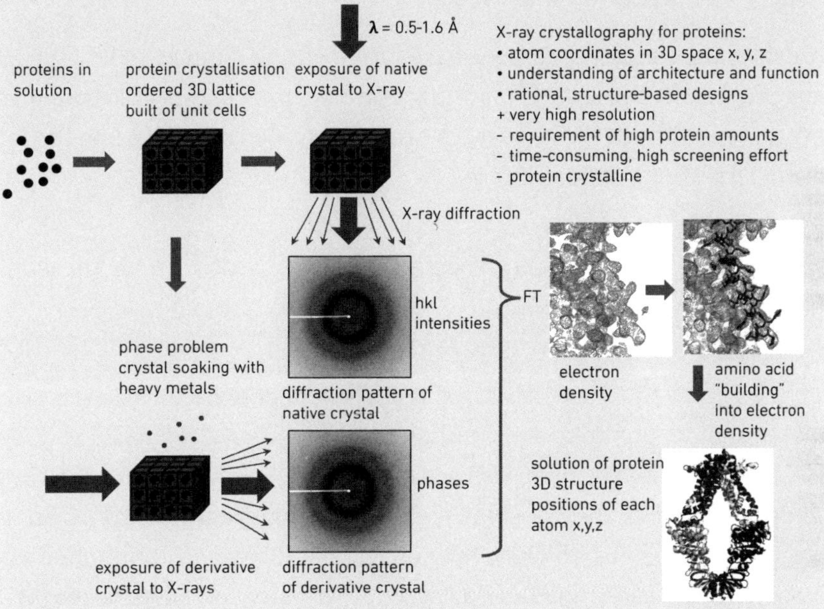

Figure 5 Advance Organizer on X-ray Crystallography.

Since the students were studying at a university of applied sciences, it was important to teach the topic in an applied manner. Although the AO represents the core statements and the most important theoretical facts of this bioanalytical method, the structure is oriented towards the experimental process. The students are therefore not only introduced to the theoretical background but can also follow the experimental procedure in the laboratory.

It can be helpful to develop an AO with chronological content, because the essential points are easier to identify than in a purely theoretical overview of a topic. Accordingly, at the beginning of the first lecture, the teacher will take the students through the AO – from left to right, then from top to bottom and again further to the right. This corresponds to the practical workflow and the information that becomes available as the work progresses.

3.4.2 Identifying key messages

An emphasis on key messages to reduce learning content to its essence has proven effective in the planning and designing stages of learning arrangements. These core messages can be identified by answering the following questions (Wüest 2017):

- What is this lesson sequence about?
- What message do I want to convey to the students with my presentation or learning activities?
- What should they remember above all?

The clarification of key messages helps teachers to define their subject material more precisely. By simultaneously defining a sequence and layout, they provide learners with a structure that simplifies access to and understanding of the context. In the following example, Prof. Claudio Nodari from the Zurich University of Teacher Education formulated key statements for each module of a degree programme for language teachers dealing with the acquisition of German as a second language.

Module 1. On second language acquisition:
"Learning a second language is like building a house and living in it at the same time."

Module 2. On vocabulary building:
"A word must be used several times in order to internalise it."

Module 3. On dealing with students' texts:
"Correction only achieves as much as the learner can consciously absorb."

Module 4. On language as a system:
"In language learning, the number of errors in texts does not decrease but remains constant as the complexity of the texts increases."

Module 5. On mental representation of the act of reading texts: "Reading is like watching a movie in your head."

These key messages are a quasi-crystallisation of the content. Starting with the core messages, the prospective teachers can reconstruct the associated concepts and examples and subsequently use them competently when preparing their lessons.

3.4.3 Encouraging students to actively engage with learning content

Not only the teachers should consider reduction. Learning is particularly effective when students actively engage with the learning content themselves. They should be able to connect new information to their own prior knowledge. They should reduce new information to its essence, for example by jotting down specific details of a presentation or a lecture or even summarizing it in their own words. In both cases, the procedure is a reductive one. When students later report to friends about the learning process or relate the most important findings back to their learning group, they also apply reduction strategies. This process involves the recognition of relationships, feedback on content, the creation of references or the development of higher-level concepts.

Teachers should actively encourage students to think about reduction possibilities. Students should be instructed to decide which specific content to keep and which to omit, giving reasons. What are the selection criteria for choosing or discarding material (reasoned selection)? They should focus on the core content (concentrating on essential elements) or simplify complex representations by means of a new, "reduced" visualisation (simplification). All three approaches are helpful. However, the reasoned selection of content is particularly helpful during the first phase of a learning process when students become easily overwhelmed by the amount and complexity of the material.

By restricting space for written information or learning time, students are forced to deal with the content of the subject matter:

Teachers, for example, can encourage students to prepare crib sheets, i.e. short summaries limited to half a page in length. They contain the most important ideas on a specific topic, thereby requiring the student to prioritise and organise course content. Teachers may also choose to let students officially use them during examinations. Those who experienced crib sheets in their own school days probably remember how useful they were: the very act of preparing crib sheets based on in-depth study of the learning material, helps the student to remember it better. It will often not be necessary to take the crib sheets into the examination itself, because actually preparing them activates processes that successfully transfer the learning material into the long-term memory.

The following exercise is an example of limiting the available time. The students are given an assignment to draft an information sheet on the completed learning process in a defined and short time span. To this end, the students write down – in a systematic manner – key messages and important terms with their definitions in a given subject area. If the teacher suggests that these documents will later be used as learning material for a subsequent group exercise, the students' motivation to prepare them usually increases.

In addition to the two basic forms of reducing available space and learning time, there are other ways of inviting participants to take part in reductive action:

1. Instruct students to draw up checklists in small groups. Students work reductively by concentrating on one aspect and defining one approach. Most of the checklists are designed for practical action and are, therefore, very popular with students. A teacher may also encourage an exchange of checklists, or the students can participate in a competition to produce the most useful and timesaving checklists.
2. Students can draft questions in an examination simulation exercise. On the one hand, we are also dealing here with content selection: students must choose a focal point. On the other hand, writing

exam questions and answers relates to an active learning technique that presupposes an intensive study of the subject matter. Experience shows that not all content can be examined equally well. However, the attempt to transform content into an exam question is a good example of a self-instructive process that promotes retention.

3. The idea sheet is another slightly more sophisticated way of encouraging students to make reductions. Here, students are asked to work on specific material in a four-step mode. The starting point is a clearly defined topic. Then, the students describe the investigated material under the headings "idea" (1), "conclusions" (2), "practical examples" or "story" (3). Under the heading "follow-up question" (4), they note whether the situation is exactly the same for similar topics. The follow-up question, which aims to transfer the results into future practice, is particularly suitable for being answered by other working groups.
4. The one-minute paper deals with the artificial limitation of time. Usually at the end of a session, students are asked to answer a maximum of two questions, in writing, within one minute. Examples of such questions are:
   - What is my take-home message today?
   - What would I like to know more about?
   - Which of my questions remain unanswered?

The advantage of this concentrated, substantive feedback is obvious: teachers find out on which level the students are, and they can identify areas in need of further action or support. At the same time, the students – before they leave the classroom – interact intensively with the subject matter and can define which gaps they would like to fill independently.

The one-minute papers can be presented if there is sufficient time. Or the teacher can collect the papers. By copying the core messages from the papers, they can be stored on a learning platform and used to create opportunities for discussion.

5. An additional form of student-driven reduction was practiced for several years in a module about language acquisition. It is based on the jigsaw technique. At the beginning of the semester, students were divided into four topic groups. The four topics covered the module content from four different perspectives. In the second to last module session, the members of the topic groups exchanged views and wrote a summary of their module content (expert group). In the last module session, groups of four were formed in which the four topics were represented (exchange groups). Based on a summary, which was sent to the module management in writing, each person presented his or her topic for ten minutes, followed by five minutes for follow-up questions. After four sessions of fifteen minutes each, the students received a form reflecting the four topics. They then had to write down keywords for the three topics they did not present themselves. Experience shows that this method is highly effective. The students were motivated to attend the module units and finally had a clear overview of the content as well as in-depth knowledge from at least one perspective.

3.5 Concluding remarks

A core task of every teacher is to define a reasoned selection of learning content and to prepare it in a way that encourages learning, so that students are able to grasp and anchor it in the available time. This chapter attempts to raise awareness for this challenge and to present reduction strategies for teachers and students alike.

Reduced to three core messages, it helps to keep the following in mind:

- Good teaching is primarily characterised by a certain quantity and presentation of learning content that is carefully attuned to the prior knowledge and performance of the students, as well as to the available time.

- Reduction of content and complexity is one of the teachers' basic tasks when planning courses; it is crucial for effective teaching and, above all, for student learning.
- Only if students actively engage with the subject matter will they be able to grasp and anchor the relevant concepts and connections.

3.6 Literature

Ammann, D. & Hermann, T. (2017). Texte meistern: Leitfaden für das Verfassen von Masterarbeiten (3rd, updated edition). Zurich: Pädagogische Hochschule Zurich (Abteilung Sekundarstufe I).

Biggs, J. & Tang, C. (2007). Teaching for quality learning at university. What the student does. Maidenhead: McGraw-Hill.

Hunter, R. (2011). Minimal lernen. Bern: hep Verlag.

Klafki, W. (1958). Didaktische Analyse als Kern der Unterrichtsvorbereitung. Die Deutsche Schule, p. 50, pp. 450-471.

Kron, F. W., Jürgens, E. & Standop, J. (2014). Grundwissen Didaktik (6th edition). Munich: Reinhardt.

Lehner, M. (2013). Viel Stoff – wenig Zeit, Wege aus der Vollständigkeitsfalle. Bern: Haupt.

Lehner, M. (2012). Didaktische Reduktion. Bern: Haupt.

Mayer, R. E. (1979). Can Advance Organizers Influence Meaningful Learning? Review of Educational Research, 49(2), pp. 371-383.

Schwengeler, C. A. & Wagner, U. A. (2002). Phänomenal: Naturbegegnung, Energie – Materie: ab 5. Schuljahr: Berner Lehrmittel- und Medienverlag.

Wüest, Y. (2017). Auf den Punkt, Didaktisch reduziert lehren und präsentieren. Zurich: Spektramedia.

Mònica Feixas & Tobias Zimmermann

4 Competence-oriented approaches to assessment

4.1 Introduction

Universities face substantial change in a rapidly evolving global society as elaborated in Chapter 1 about the redefinition of higher education. The challenges of meeting new expectations about academic standards in the next decade and beyond mean that assessment needs to be continuously rethought and renewed. Enhancing assessment in higher education involves systematic planning in order to provide assessment tasks that require the integration of knowledge and development of competences.

This includes expanding the view of assessment towards being a self-regulated learning activity for students. If we want assessments to contribute to a productive learning and teaching culture, students have to take on responsibility for their own assessment process and self-regulation of learning (and that of their peers). This is not easy, but necessary and possible if the right measures are taken. This chapter considers different perspectives of assessment and takes a stand on improving assessment practices by promoting formative activities that aim at fostering the students' learning.

The first part starts by clarifying the concept of assessment, the main purposes of assessment and the differences between assessment of, assessment for and assessment as learning. It proposes that assessment as learning – assessment to foster learning throughout life – be given equal attention alongside the well-established assessment for learning and assessment of learning. It proceeds with an examination of the formats, methods and tools of assessment in formal settings, combined with some questions of quality and reliability regarding assessment procedures. The final part of the chapter focuses on the moments and agents of assessment and delves into topics such as the building of rubrics for assessment, avoiding plagiarism and accounting for the heterogeneity of students' learning strategies in the assessment design.

4.2 Conceptualisation of assessment – what is assessment?

Where do we want students to be at the end of a course or degree programme? And, most importantly, how will we know if they get there? The answers to these two questions will lead us to think of assessment as a key process of collecting information about student learning and performance to improve education. Assessment can be conceived as the art and science of knowing what students know, or the process that aims to provide useful information about whether students have reached important learning objectives and, therefore, about the progress of each student. Huba and Freed (2000) define assessment as:

"the process of gathering and discussing information from multiple and diverse sources in order to develop a deep understanding of what students know, understand, and can do with their knowledge as a result of their educational experiences; the process culminates when assessment results are used to improve subsequent learning (p. 8)."

As far as assessment terminology is concerned, there are some subtle differences between the terms criticise, assess, grade/mark and evaluate:

- **Criticise:** to give somebody feedback on a piece of work,
- **Assess:** to gather data as we hear or see the student or read his/her work in order to foster his/her learning process,
- **Mark/Grade:** to give a value for the level of achievement measured against specified criteria for an individual assessment item or for a period of learning,
- **Evaluate:** to give somebody feedback, make judgments and assign a value to a piece of work.

The actual conceptualisation of assessment can be sustained by the following underpinning principles:

1. Assessment is a central feature of teaching and the curriculum. It powerfully drives how students learn and what students achieve. It is one of the most significant influences on students' experience of higher education, on the student perceptions of the curriculum and the ways in which they may engage in processes to acquire skills (Boud & Associates, 2010).
2. Assessment is a challenging activity because of all the decisions teachers face about students' learning. Whereas some of these decisions may seem small and inconsequential, others are "high stakes" influencing the life course of students, e.g. decisions about how to best teach and train students for academic and professional life. In addition, the misalignment of assessment practices to learning objectives, the impact of negative feedback or the making of subjective judgements not based on evidence, etc. can affect learning results.
3. Assessment is not only the final outcome or end result of teaching and learning activities. It is, by contrast, fundamental to teaching and learning in order to test students' aptitudes as well as to prepare and motivate them in their learning. Assessment is therefore just as crucial 'for' and 'as' learning as it is 'of' learning. This is necessary to ensure that the intended learning outcomes may be achieved in keeping with the higher education standards and benchmarks.
4. Student assessment is viewed by teachers and students differently; for the teachers, assessment is the final consideration in the design of the teaching and learning process (after the planning of the content, teaching and learning methods and resources), whereas for students, it is usually at the forefront of their minds (Figure 1).

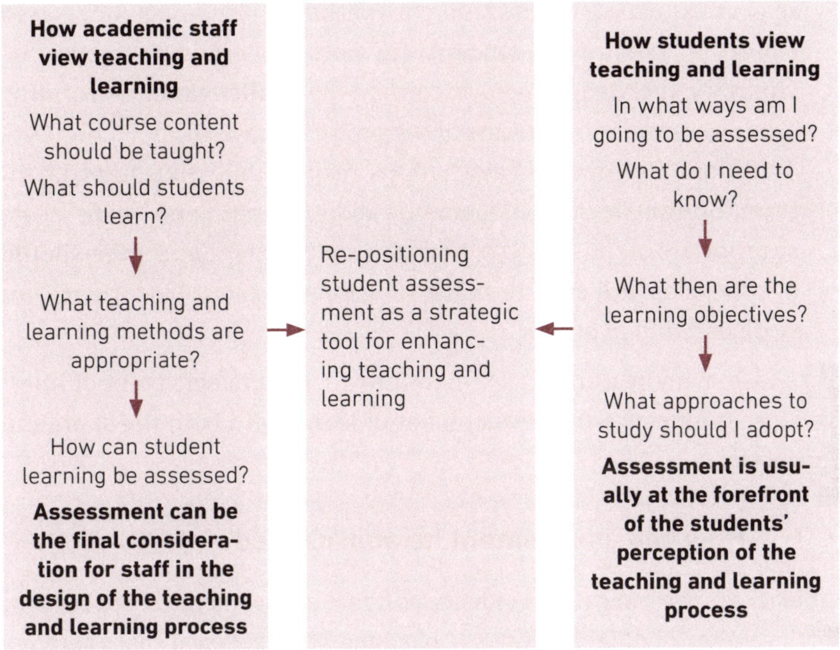

Figure 1 Views on assessment by teachers and students (Biggs 2003).

5. Although assessment in higher education focuses on individual students, it does so in the context of the other students in a particular course, their degree programme, the institution and the national education system. Thus, it is necessary to understand the curricular requirements and standards of all of these factors when embarking on assessment formats, criteria, marking and feedback. Assessment is a holistic process that needs to permeate all aspects of teaching, learning and assessment (Biggs 2003). In addition, the notion of constructive alignment (cf. Chapter 2, section 2.9) must be extended to encompass not only consistency of purpose between the elements of programmes, but to plan and seek its impact on long-term purposes beyond graduation (Feixas & Zellweger 2018).
6. Assessment includes many factors that influence its effectiveness. Among others, these factors include accountability and student readiness, catering for diversity and addressing fairness, assessing

relevant knowledge and skills, concentrating on competency-based education to equip the students for work and exposure to interdisciplinary knowledge and overcoming the challenges of performing group assessments in terms of the group's composition.

7. Traditionally, teachers have had the responsibility of gathering information and making judgements about how students' work meets appropriate standards, but nowadays students themselves should also develop the skill to make judgements about both their own work and that of others.

For these many reasons, assessment provides a strategic point of intervention to influence the development of learning in both the short and long term.

4.3 How can assessment be approached?

As teachers, we can gather evidence and make judgements about student achievement in different ways. It has long been believed that there are two main purposes of assessment: summative and formative.

- The summative purpose is to provide certification of achievement. Certification is a validated record of a student's performance in a certain programme; it is typically used by employers and by educational institutions to make judgements about acceptability for employment or further study.
- The formative purpose is to facilitate learning. Feedback from various kinds of assignments enables students to judge their own achievements and what they need to do to learn more effectively within the programme.

These two purposes have been associated with different sets of practices (Earl & Katz 2006):

- Assessment **of** learning: this helps teachers in using evidence of student learning to assess achievement against outcomes and standards. Sometimes referred to as 'summative assessment', it usually occurs at defined key points during a unit of learning or at the end of such a unit, term or semester and may be used to mark or grade students.

- Assessment **for** learning: teachers use evidence about students' knowledge, understanding and skills to inform their teaching. Sometimes referred to as 'formative assessment', it usually occurs throughout the teaching and learning process to clarify student learning and understanding.
- Assessment **as** learning: this occurs when students are their own assessors. Students monitor their own learning, ask questions and use a range of strategies to decide what they know and can do and how to use assessment for new learning.

Summative assessment is used to judge which competences the student leaves the module or programme with, i.e. whether or not the student has met the respective learning outcomes of the course. In order to do so, the type of summative task and the assessment criteria need to be aligned with the course content and learning outcomes. As an assessment **of** learning, summative assessment is judgmental in order to communicate the achievements of the students to external parties; it can also form part of both continuous and integrated assessments.

Summative assessment serves to validate the attainment of a certain level of education. Thus, summative assessment usually occurs at specific moments or end-points of a module / term / semester / programme. The results are used to decide on progression or promotion to the next semester or level, or even employment. Students are aware that the given task is for summative purposes; the task is usually a structured process of a formal nature such as a written test, drawing assignment, portfolio exam, term paper or thesis.

Summative assessment can also be employed as part of continuous assessment, if the assessment is an on-going process that measures a learner's achievements in a course of study on a particular level. This way, it provides information that can be used to support a learner's development and to improve the learning and teaching process.

Formative assessment encourages students to take responsibility for their learning by adequately equipping them to form opinions about their abilities, to construct their own knowledge and to set their own goals. Because formative assessment takes place during the programme – and thereby within the process of learning and teaching – it is considered as assessment **for** learning; it facilitates students' learning and acts as a learning tool in preparation for summative assessment. Thus, to prepare students for the summative assessment, constructive feedback should be provided promptly in the form of individual and group feedback. This feedback does not have to be provided by the teacher alone but can also be given by peers. It can take the form of written comments specific to each student's work, as well as a general discussion in class. Most importantly, it allows students to engage with the feedback and evaluate the tasks through critical dialogue and/or peer review, thereby encouraging both self and peer assessment and development.

Assessment **as** learning involves both teachers and students setting learning objectives to encourage growth and development. It requires students to ask questions and take on responsibility for their learning, encourages peer assessment and provides ways for students to use formal and informal feedback and self-assessment to help them understand the next steps in learning. It is possible to combine both formative and summative elements into an assessment culture that understands assessment primarily as a chance to inform about learning and development.

The three approaches to assessment work quite well together. Nevertheless, the principles of assessment **for** learning and assessment **as** learning are more appropriate for helping teachers and students to decide whether students are ready for the next phase of learning, or whether they need further learning experiences to consolidate their knowledge, understanding and skills.

4.3.1 Reference standards

When assessing a student, we need some kind of scale or agreed-upon standards. The standards set the criteria for the successful demonstration of the understanding of a concept or skill. In this respect, we distinguish between three different reference standards:

- **Individual reference standard:** The performance of a student is measured against his/her personal development. Has he/she improved or deteriorated with regard to a specific learning objective or competence compared to earlier performances?
- **Criterion-based reference standard:** The performances of students are measured against pre-defined learning objectives (competences). These have to be defined as clearly and as transparently as possible (cf. Chapter 2) and make it possible to classify a measured performance on a certain scale, i.e. how well does a certain performance meet the previously defined criteria?
- **Social reference standard:** Student performances are compared within a certain group (e.g. class or cohort). How large is the deviation of the individual performance from the average of the peer group? Here, a content-related reference standard is also needed, but the scale is not calibrated by estimating the degree of difficulty but solely to form a ranking. The definition of which percentage of students is attributed which performance level remains arbitrary and is not content-related.

While the first two reference standards are important and useful, the social reference standard is not appropriate for educational use because the distribution of performance levels in a student class is basically random. For example, it is likely that students from different years of the degree course do not perform exactly equally well. If each year, 60% of a cohort pass an assessment whereas 40% do not, students who perform equally well with regard to a criterion-based reference standard would pass this assessment in one year, but not in the other. This is not fair and should be avoided whenever possible.

4.3.2 Some remarks on summative assessment and grading

Summative assessment is usually graded, be it with numerical or letter grades (e.g. 1-6 or A-F). However, there is a broad consensus in educational diagnostics that grading with numbers or letters is highly problematic and should be abolished (cf. Ingenkamp & Lissmann 2008, Sacher 2014, and Winter 2012). This is due to the fact that numerical and letter grades have serious disadvantages compared to more elaborate feedback on student performance (be it in writing or oral):

- They suggest an exact measurability and comparability of performances. Thus, an unrealistic accuracy and differentiation is presumed (cf. section 4.5.1 below "Criteria for assessing"). In contrast, numerous studies show that the grades students receive depend to a much greater extent on the particular student cohort or class they attend than on their actual individual performance level (Ingenkamp & Lissmann 2008, pp. 137-155). Therefore, numerical and letter grades do not comply with the quality criteria for assessments that are explained below (see section 4.5.2 "Quality of assessments").
- Grades do not give any details about content: which competences have been acquired to what extent, and where is there still room for improvement? To answer these questions in a more differentiated manner, preferably written feedback is necessary. Furthermore, the simultaneous announcement of numerical or letter grades with differentiated verbal feedback has been shown to weaken the perception and thereby the effect of the feedback (Gibbs & Simpson 2004, p. 23f.).

Of course, so-called basic grades (cf. Sacher 2014, p. 99) are indispensable. These are roughly graded judgments such as above average – average – below average (social reference standard), improvement – consistent performance – deterioration (individual reference standard), outperforming – fulfilling – failing or pass – fail (both criterion-based reference standards). To come up with such ratings is an essential component of summative but also of formative assessment – especially based on individual or criterion reference standards. Such ratings have to meet at least the following requirements (Sacher 2014, pp. 99-101):

- The allocation of the grades has to be well defined. Equal performances always have to be given the same grades. However, the identical grades can be given to varying performances because grades always combine a certain performance range. If 100 students are assessed, there can be 100 different performances, but if there are only three predicates, then there can be only three different grades.
- The allocation of grades has to be compatible with the reference standard. Only characteristics that are relevant to the chosen reference standard should be measured. For example, a criterion-based grading cannot be changed after marking simply because one feels that too many students would receive a good grade.
- The allocation of grades has to be error-controlled. This means that while giving grades, teachers should be aware of potential measurement errors, and they should try to reduce them as far as possible.

These requirements underlie both the formulation of written/oral assessments and the calculation of grades, the latter often being a mandatory task for university teachers (despite all the weaknesses of grading mentioned above). The mathematical and test-theoretical details of quantifying student performances and of allocating grades cannot be expounded here for reasons of space. For a comprehensive explanation, see ETH Zurich, Educational Development and Technology 2013 or Sacher 2014, pp. 101-127.

4.4 What to assess? Assessment of competences

The learning objectives determine what is to be assessed (cf. Chapter 2 "Formulating learning outcomes"). Assessments should therefore offer a statement about which learning objectives have been reached and to what extent, i.e. which competences and competence levels students have achieved. At the same time, it is important that assessments indicate in which areas and in what ways students can enhance their competences. This necessitates formats of assessments that go beyond recalling memorised information, in which students, for example:

- learn to assess their own performances and those of their peers (self and peer assessment),
- learn to develop assessments or assignments of tasks themselves,
- work cooperatively on an assessment (group assessments, peer coaching, etc.).

In this respect, it is essential that students receive feedback (from teachers, peers or software) in different ways to inform themselves about their learning performances and their handling of the assignments (see the section 4.6.2 "Formative feedback" below).

4.4.1 Assessment of competences

When learning objectives are formulated as competences to be acquired, assessment of performance should not be reduced to testing if students have learned the subject matter off by heart and are able to reproduce it as accurately as possible. Unfortunately, such tests of memory are still common in many places, but they only cover the lowest level of Bloom's taxonomy of educational objectives (cf. Chapter 2, section 2.4). Rather, assessments should strive to make the competences that are defined by the learning objectives visible. Thus, beyond remembering and understanding knowledge, skills such as applying, analysing, evaluating and creating should be targeted by assessments. In this regard, transfer tasks are important (see Figure 2). Transfer tasks require students to tackle a problem that has not already been addressed or solved in exactly the same way, be it during class or in an exercise or homework assignment (cf. Metzger & Nüesch 2004, pp. 17-21).

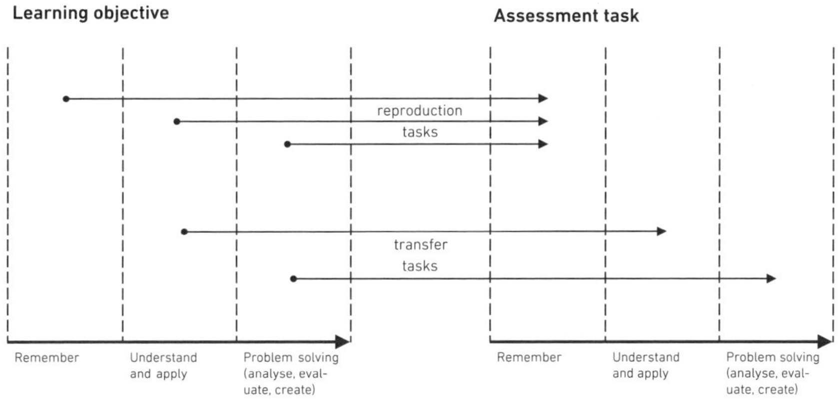

Figure 2 Reproduction vs. transfer tasks (based on Metzger & Nüesch 2004, p. 17f.).

One possible format to assess competences is the "two-phase or two-stage exam". A two-phase exam combines the assessment and accountability virtues of a traditional individual exam with the learning benefits and rapid formative feedback of a group problem-solving process (Wieman et al., 2018). First, during the solo phase, students work through the exam individually. Then they turn in their answer sheets, are assigned to groups for the team phase and collaborate to complete the exam (or a subset or variation of it) a second time. Two-phase exams are intended to make students articulate their thinking with their teammates, explore each other's reasoning, resolve differences and agree on a mutually satisfactory answer.

To create assessments that really address the desired taxonomy level, it is helpful to ask the following questions (cf. Brown et al. 1997, p. 49):

1. What and on which level are the learning objectives to be assessed?
2. Is the assessment strategy compatible with the learning objectives?
3. Are the chosen formats relatively efficient in terms of student time and staff time?
4. What alternatives are there? What are their advantages and disadvantages?

5. Does the specific assessment task match the outcomes and skills?
6. Are the marking schemes or criteria appropriate?

These questions help to find appropriate formats and suitable criteria to check the extent to which students have reached the learning objectives. It is also important that students can practice such tasks before the actual assessment takes place.

4.4.2 How to assess higher-order thinking skills

The congruence of learning objectives, teaching and learning methods and assessment tasks is essential. Not every task, not every assessment format is suitable for every level of educational objectives. For example, using case studies as the main teaching and learning method is not congruent with assessing students' learning of the course with one final multiple-choice test at the end of the semester. Therefore, Figure 3 gives an overview of levels of educational objectives, suitable teaching and learning activities and possible assessment formats.

Taxonomy of learning objectives	Matching activity	Assessment format	
Creating	Make, build, write, design something new (e.g. essays, business plans, research projects, performances, designs)	Complex case study, final paper (bachelor/ master/ doctoral thesis), exploratory laboratory work	divergent
Evaluating	Test, monitor, evaluate, criticise complex subject matter such as products, texts, performances against criteria/standards	Longer paper, portfolio, comprehensive project documentation / evaluation	
Analysing	Discriminate relevant aspects of a case, project, concept, etc. Determine how different parts, aspects, elements are connected with one another	Short paper, small project, concept map, learning diary	type of performance (tendency!): ↕
Applying	Apply procedures to more or less structured tasks Determine the most appropriate procedures for a given task	Oral exam, written online discussion, simple case study, laboratory tasks	
Understanding	Summarise, paraphrase, classify, compare elements (texts, theories, cases...)	Presentation, elaboration, group or class discussion, minutes	convergent
Remembering	Recall or recognise definitions and facts, mainly from learning materials	Recall test such as multiple choice, fill-in-the-blank, answering closed questions	

Figure 3 Competence levels, matching activities and assessment formats (based on Iller & Wick 2009 and Eberly Center 2008/2015).

The transitions between different levels are not completely mutually exclusive. For example, a concept map can also be part of a complex case study, and a multiple-choice (MC) test can also address the objective level of understanding/organising if the MC items are well formulated. However, there are limits: even the best MC test barely makes it possible to assess competence levels such as evaluating or even creating.

Moreover, the figure is a further illustration of the difference between reproduction and transfer tasks, which was presented in the previous section.

Example: Reproduction vs. transfer task

Learning objective: Students can develop assessment formats and tasks that are adequate for the targeted competency level.

Reproduction task: List the reference standards for assessment. What are they suitable for, and what are their advantages and disadvantages? (This task aims at reproducing knowledge taught in the course; at best it targets the learning objective level of understanding.)

Transfer task: A colleague who is teaching a course at university for the first time asks you for advice: her students have to learn the basics of ethical argumentation. How can she best assess if students are able to argue based on ethical principles? Explain to her what challenges she is facing and suggest an assessment format that you think is suitable for her situation. (This task aims at transferring knowledge about assessment to a new situation and targets the learning objective levels of analysing, evaluating and creating.)

4.5 How to assess? Criteria, tools and procedures

4.5.1 Criteria for assessing

To determine the qualities of a student product or performance (written or oral statements, artistic works, practical activities, etc.) is not at all trivial. Assessment criteria are necessary, and they have to be weighted.

However, not all criteria can be formulated in an equally unambiguous manner so everybody understands them in the same way. Therefore, different assessors who evaluate the same performances according to the same criteria can reach fairly diverging findings. In order to reduce such inter-subjective differences, the use of assessment criteria can be optimised by calibration procedures (cf. Sadler 2013). However, even the best calibration cannot eliminate inter-subjective differences completely; performance assessments always involve some degree of uncertainty or fuzziness. Thus, we advise against using overly complicated grading scales or finely tuned grades, since they neither help to meet vital quality criteria nor do they help to avoid cognitive bias (see following sections).

Based on these challenges, we recommend paying attention to the following list of essential ideas when designing and using assessment criteria:

- "match the assessment task and learning outcome,
- enable consistency of marking,
- identify areas of disagreement between assessors,
- help students to achieve the learning outcomes,
- get used to provide useful feedback to students" (Brown 2001, p. 16).

An example of a fully developed assessment scenario that addresses these demands can be found in Figure 6, section 4.9.

4.5.2 Quality of assessments

In order to be meaningful, performance assessments have to meet certain quality criteria. We differentiate between the following three vital psychometric criteria of objectivity, reliability and validity (cf. Ingenkamp & Lissmann 2008, pp. 51-61):

- **Objectivity** (independence): A measurement is more objective the more the measurement results are independent of the person doing the measuring. If a measurement is objective, different persons should get the same result when measuring the same feature. However, objectivity is only ever approximately attainable – a measurement is never absolutely independent from the person(s) doing the measuring (see also the section on cognitive bias below).

- **Reliability** (measuring accuracy): The more exactly and reliably a measurement quantifies a certain feature, the higher its reliability. As in the case of objectivity, this is not an absolute criterion either, since a measurement cannot be more reliable than the stability of the feature to be measured (cf. Ingenkamp & Lissmann 2008, p. 55). And indeed, performances of students vary, e.g. depending on the time of day or the general stress level of a person. Different ways of measuring performance may cause variations, too. For instance, one student may be skilful in expressing herself orally but have difficulties expressing herself in writing. Therefore, she will probably perform better in an oral exam than in an essay, even though her competence regarding the subject matter is the same.
- **Validity** (validness): A performance measurement is valid if it actually measures what it is supposed to measure, and not something else. If a measurement does not measure what it claims to, it is simply not valid. This may sound trivial at first, but it is the most fundamental of the quality criteria for performance assessments (cf. Ingenkamp & Lissmann 2008, p. 57, and Sacher 2014, pp. 35–41). For instance, if an assessment is conducted under time pressure, it does not only test subject-related competences but also to a considerable extent the ability to act under stress and to make fast decisions. In some professional contexts, this may make sense (e.g. to test if health care specialists are ready to work in an emergency room), but for most contexts it does not. The same holds true regarding the still widespread closed-book tests; they are good for measuring rote learning but far from ideal for measuring more complex competences. Therefore, the circumstances and the context in which an assessment is conducted are very important, too.

There are some conflicts between validity on the one hand and objectivity and reliability on the other hand (cf. Metzger & Nüesch, p. 9). If the learning objectives aim at higher-order thinking skills, the assessment tasks have to be transfer-oriented (cf. section 4.4.1 "Assessment of competences" above) and, thus, are more complex than simple reproduction tasks. But the more complex a task is, the harder it is to correct reliably and objectively, i.e. to avoid measurement errors and subjectivity. Therefore, the more complex assessment tasks are, the more important it is to take measures to minimise measurement errors and subjective bias. Possible answers are detailed rubrics (cf. section 4.5.4 "Rubrics" below), calibrating correctors or correction by two different persons. If weighting of the criteria is necessary, e.g. for economical reasons, then validity should be weighted highest (although traditionally, the contrary is more likely to happen, not least because authorities dealing with appeals – and also students themselves – instinctively tend to focus on objectivity and reliability).

4.5.3 Cognitive bias

However important the quality criteria are, it has to be noted that competences can never be observed directly but only indirectly – by way of written or spoken statements or, in some cases, physical actions. These statements or actions have to be perceived and interpreted, and only the interpretations can be assessed. During these operations, cognitive bias is likely to cause certain distortions (cf. Hilbert 2012), resulting in errors of assessment.

A typical error of assessment is caused by the choice of unsuitable indicators. For example, the frequency of a student's contributions to class discussions does not allow conclusions as to his/her learning commitment (e.g. a more valid indicator would be voluntary engagement with the subject matter in the student's free time). In the following list, we present a small selection of "classical" types of cognitive bias that are relevant to assessment (cf. Greve & Wentura 1997, pp. 56-74):

- **Tendency towards the mean:** Extreme judgements are avoided (e.g. teachers that hardly ever give the best or the worst grades).
- **Tendency towards the extreme:** Judgments in the centre of a scale are avoided (e.g. teachers that divide students quite radically into "good" and "bad" students).
- **Halo effect:** Based on certain indicators, conclusions about other characteristics of a student are drawn in a judgmental way (e.g. a person that is often absent is either not interested or lazy).
- **Reference error:** An unsuitable reference standard is chosen (e.g. the performance rank within a cohort of students instead of objective criteria such as learning objectives that were communicated in advance; see the remarks on reference standards earlier in this chapter).
- **Serial position effect:** There is always a more or less large time interval between an observation and a judgement or assessment. Out of a series of stimuli, we tend to remember the first and the last particularly well (e.g. an especially good/bad last part of an oral exam can skew the assessment considerably).

4.5.4 Rubrics

Assessment rubrics are matrices that include different performance dimensions and several performance levels, both of which are clearly defined or described in writing. They can characterise the quality of students' performances in a differentiated manner on the one hand, and on the other hand they facilitate self and peer assessments of/by students (cf. Sluijsmans et al. 2006, pp. 50–55). Thus, rubrics are an important assessment instrument that allows teachers to meet the requirements formulated by Brown (2001) in the section 4.5.1 "Criteria for assessing"; they can be used for formative as well as summative assessments.

If assessment rubrics are already made transparent at the beginning of a course or if they are even developed together with the students, they make students continuously aware of what they already know and where there is still potential for development.

A central feature of rubrics is their orientation to the qualities of students' performances. Thus, they are not oriented towards deficiencies or mistakes – rather, every additional quality that is shown in a student's performance leads to a better assessment (see Figure 4). This has a positive effect on students' motivation: they are expected to show what they can do, not to primarily avoid making mistakes. Moreover, rubrics facilitate giving feedback, for teachers as well as for peers.

	Excellent	Proficient	Fair	Inadequate
Problem statement/ Hypothesis	Problem statement is clearly articulated and well debated in the opening and concluding sections of the essay.	Problem statement is debated and is evident in the argument but is not clearly articulated.	Problem statement is unclear, and it takes work for the reader to extract it out of the text. Or, the problem statement is self-evident but not debated.	There is no evident problem statement.
Argumentation	Argument is presented clearly and logically. Logical points build directly upon the problem statement and prior points. Counter arguments are addressed, dismantled, and folded into the main argument of the paper.	Argument is presented clearly and logically, but points do not necessarily build on each other. Counter arguments are addressed, but many are left hanging or are dealt with inadequately.	Argument is rambling, and there are contradictions left unaddressed. Counter arguments may have been presented but are left unaddressed.	There is no discernible argument, or no alternative interpretation is presented.
Etc.	(...)	(...)	(...)	(...)

Figure 4 Rubric used for grading an analytical essay in sociology (excerpt from Gaston 2011).

4.5.5 Avoiding plagiarism

Pressure on students can tempt them to plagiarise. In the age of mobile Internet, information is so accessible that the temptation to simply copy grows. Many universities have nowadays installed programs that check for plagiarism. But from an educational perspective, this is only a sensible approach if students can check their texts themselves and are supported in drawing the right conclusions from the results. Apart from monitoring and punishment, the most important strategy in avoiding plagiarism is prevention. This can be achieved on different levels:

- Setting assignments that limit the opportunities for plagiarism. For example, critically analysing various recent articles or using last week's newspaper articles,
- Spending sufficient time informing students about the precise nature of the assessment criteria that will be used, for example in the form of rubrics (see above). Are you rewarding students for merely finding information or for analysing and evaluating it? The latter reduces the risk of plagiarism,
- Involving students in the design of assessment tasks and in the setting of assessment criteria gives them a feeling of inclusion and ownership and promotes a more positive attitude to learning (Ion, Barrera & Tomàs 2016),
- Teaching students what paraphrasing and citations are, how they are formulated and where plagiarism starts. Supporting students' writing and giving formative feedback during the writing phase of longer papers/theses are most helpful, too.

4.6 When to assess?

4.6.1 Moments: before, during and after

As a process, assessment takes place at different moments, for different purposes and poses different levels of "risk" for the students:

- **Diagnostic assessment or pre-assessment** provides information about **what the student has already learned** and enables teachers to make initial evidenced-based decisions about instructional planning (objectives; teaching, learning and assessment methods),
- **Progress monitoring assessment** provides evidence of progress toward standards **several times during the semester/year**. These assessments are sometimes used in a summative manner to document student growth, but the data they provide can often be used formatively to modify instruction during the next learning unit or semester, etc.,
- **Final assessment** is retrospective and "summarises" what students have learned, i.e. to what extent they have acquired the competences as defined in the learning outcomes of the module.

Figure 5 shows a synthesis of some examples of assessment tools that can be used at these different moments:

Moments When do you assess?	Stakes What is the level of risk for students?	Purposes Why assess?	Examples How do you assess?
DIAGNOSTIC / INITIAL (before teaching to determine what student already knows)	• low • no grade given	• to gather data and diagnose students' knowledge and skills before a new period of learning starts • to plan for instruction • as student, to assess one's own knowledge and skills to inform/guide the upcoming learning activities	• concept map • quiz or test • task • application of skills • reflection

Moments When do you assess?	Stakes What is the level of risk for students?	Purposes Why assess?	Examples How do you assess?
PROGRESS MONITORING / CONTINU-OUS (while teach-ing to also give students opportunities to self-reg-ulate their learning)	• low • no grade given unless formative leads to summative	• to gather data and give feedback • to monitor or ad-just instruction • as students, to monitor • and self-regulate learning tasks	• review quiz or test • portfolio • conference • journal, log • role play • observation check list • peer review • reflection (combined with student, peer and teacher checklists and rubrics)
FINAL (after teaching for culminating evaluation)	• high • grade given	• to gather data and evaluate • to make decisions regarding grades, promotion, grad-uation	• test/exam • portfolio • demonstration of a competence in an authentic situation (i.e. work experience) • presentation • project • reflection (combined with teacher and possi-bly student or peer evaluative check-lists and rubrics)

Figure 5 Moments, stakes, purposes and tools for assessment.

The assessment "during", i.e. progress monitoring, is especially important because it is the moment for giving formative feedback to students and involving them in this task. Why is feedback so relevant?

4.6.2 Formative feedback: a reciprocal endeavour

Feedback is a key component of the learning and assessment activity for the reflective construction of knowledge (Hounsell 2008). But feedback may also be given reciprocally by groups of students or peers. According to Hattie (2009), feedback is one of the most important factors influencing what students really learn. The purposes of feedback are to motivate students, to inform them how well they have done and how to improve. These purposes should be set within the framework of the learning outcomes, the assignment requirements and the assessment criteria that are being used. Traditionally, feedback includes qualitative comments given from the teacher to a student or a group of students.

The greater part of the time for assessing students should be spent on giving feedback. The challenge is to give formative and constructive feedback to a large number of students. In this regard, some strategies are available for managing large numbers of students and saving time, yet providing useful feedback to students. They are essentially: reduce the assessment load, streamline the feedback procedure and – most important – delegate at least a significant portion of giving feedback to the students themselves. When feedback emphasises not only the information about the current learning process but also the actions and strategies to promote learning throughout life, we talk about "feedforward" (Ion, Barrera & Tomàs 2016).

In fact, Hounsell (2003) suggests that we should move in the direction of "student involvement in the generation of feedback, and a more open and collaborative approach to assignments" (p. 78). This is the idea behind assessment AS learning, where students are their own assessors. Students on their own or with peers can learn to monitor their own learning, ask themselves questions and use a range of strategies to examine what they know and can do and how to use assessment for new learning. One approach is to develop effective assessment criteria together with students, for example in the form of a rubric to assess oral presentation skills. Several groups of students use it to assess the oral presentation of a group project. Each group of students provides a mark for every presentation. The final grade takes into account the class' average and the teacher's mark. Thereby, the teacher with the students (individually or in groups) can judge a given learning activity and provide joint feedback.

4.7 Who can assess? Teacher, external, self-assessment and peer assessment

Teachers can be best placed to make judgments on specialist subject knowledge, but there are others who could also be involved in the assessment process: employers (external assessment), other students (peer assessment) or the student him/herself (self-assessment). Employers can assess as part of a work placement course (especially in further education settings), but generally their role is limited. However, other options are plausible in daily teaching. If the main goal of an assessment is to provide formative feedback, we can consider students assessing each other. Peer assessment is regarded as a very positive source of feedback because students usually respond better to the feedback provided by peers (De Grez, Valcke & Roozen 2012). Self-assessment is also useful to check on the learning acquired and, given an adequate tool (survey, check-list, reflective portfolio or other sorts of guidelines), is a pre-requisite for self-regulation of learning and personal and professional growth.

Self-assessment and peer assessment are not methods of assessment but sources of assessment data and could be used with any method or instrument. Peer and self-assessment can be used for both formative and/or summative assessment. Their use in formative assessment is more common, perhaps due to concerns surrounding validity and reliability if students are allowed to award summative grades to themselves or their peers. However, even when not used directly in summative assessment, peer and self-assessment can inform a teacher's summative marking, e.g. when assessing group work. Thus peer and self-assessment of a group project may be a useful way of encouraging students to reflect upon their own learning process, the teamwork process and the final product. Explicit criteria should be used to ensure consistency and fairness. Nevertheless, final-year marks based solely on self-assessment and implicit criteria would, for most of us, seem totally inappropriate.

4.8 Assessing students with special educational needs and disabilities (SEND)

Commitment to inclusivity means recognising and valuing our diverse student body and taking measures to improve the success of specific groups, including students with special educational needs and disabilities (SEND). Since the Salamanca Declaration, which specifically advocated for the provision of 'mainstream' education for students with disabilities (UNESCO 1994), significant progress has been made. But still, there are many barriers to learning to overcome, such as effects of an impairment or medical condition, physical environment, availability and effectiveness of educational support, teaching style, teachers' attitudes and relations with SEND students and assessment methods. In fact, both assessments and course work present special problems. Some of the difficulties concern access to learning resources or the physical environment of SEND students, the rates at which they process information and their capacity to communicate their learning.

Inclusive assessment does not compromise academic standards but improves the chances for all students to demonstrate their ability to meet the learning outcomes. It is more time-effective and fair to consider the inclusiveness of the assessment in the programme or module design phase, rather than making individual adjustments later in the programme (Hockings 2010). In addition, inclusive assessment helps to avoid the assumption that certain groups of students have a particular way of learning, when in reality students with disabilities "fall along a continuum of learner differences and share similar challenges and difficulties that all students face in higher education" (Healey et al. 2006, p. 41).

In order to assess inclusively, we should introduce flexibility as to how students demonstrate their knowledge and use a variety of assessment formats (e.g. presentation, lab. report, reflective portfolio). Other considerations include allowing choice in assignments (e.g. choice of topic or letting students set their own questions), designing inclusive exams and considering how technology can assist. Plymouth University's (2014)

"7 steps" give practical guidance and tips to incorporate inclusive assessment into modules and programmes.

4.9 Designing an assessment approach

Designing assessment is the process at the micro level of setting the assessment formats, criteria, marking and feedback as part of constructive alignment according to the following aspects:

- the aims of the overall programme,
- the learning objectives of the module or course,
- the content selection,
- the methods of teaching and learning.

As an example, we show an assessment approach based on an optional 4.5 ECTS course on "Art and Anthropology" for 3rd year Bachelor students in humanities (Figure 6). The approach takes into consideration various learning activities, moments of assessment, period of the semester (or week when the assignment is due), whether optional or mandatory, the agent (or who is performing the assessment), whether individual, peer or group assessment and the percentage allocated to this activity in the overall assessment.

Figure 6 is an example of a specification table for planning assessments. It summarises the "what to assess", "who can assess" (teacher, peers), "when to assess" (moments: initial phase, during the semester or final phase), "how to assess", the week(s) in which the assessment activity will take place and the weighting of each activity. It also indicates that assessment activities can involve individual students, small groups or the whole class and that the teacher has the opportunity to choose whether the assessment activity is mandatory or optional. Here, some assessment activities are optional; these give the students some degrees of freedom within the overall assessment, which is important for their motivation and autonomy.

Learning activity/task WHAT?	Sort of assessment task WHEN?	Period of time (week)	Kind of activity WHAT FOR?	Optional/ mandatory	Agent of evaluation WHO?	Students' grouping HOW?	% HOW MUCH?
Activity 1. Written summary of the museum visit	Initial	1/11	Introductory	Optional	Teacher/ Self-assessment	Individual	10%
Activity 2. Analysis of aesthetic art work	Continuous	5,6,8	Application	Mandatory	Teacher	Pairs	15%
Act. 3. Oral presentation	Continuous	6,7,8	Application & conceptual	Mandatory	Teacher/ Peer assessment	Small group	10%
Act. 4. Critical opinion through in-class debate	Continuous	6,7,8	Application, conceptual & synthesis	Optional	Teacher	Whole class	15%
Activity 5. Portfolio: drawing project	Continuous	7-10	Application, conceptual & synthesis	Mandatory	Teacher/ Peer assessment	Small group	25%
Activity 6. Written and oral tests	Final	11	Application, conceptual & synthesis	Mandatory	Teacher/ Self-assessment	Individual	25% **=100%**

Figure 6 An example of assessment planning for a 4.5 ECTS optional course on Art and Anthropology (Bachelor's Degree in Humanities) (own elaboration).

Beyond the table, some additional information sets the framework for the course:

The context:
The course engages the knowledge dimensions (ranging from concrete to abstract knowledge) at various intensities as appropriate to specific teaching and learning activities and outcomes: factual knowledge, e.g. basic elements and terminology (jargon) in art and anthropology, which the students must know in order to understand and work within the arts discipline; conceptual knowledge, e.g. theories, classifications and principles behind art and anthropology; procedural knowledge, e.g. critical thinking skills and specific methods of enquiry necessary for research design. To ensure the effectiveness of assessments, an approach to assessment is developed that includes the balance of theory and practical components in order to meet the different levels of learning outcomes. The assessment tasks should also be aligned with learning outcomes and pitched at an appropriate level of complexity by incorporating the suitable level descriptors as well as addressing the cognitive complexities of Bloom's revised taxonomy.

Moments of assessment:
A visit to the museum, for example, addresses the diversity of student knowledge by testing the students' ability to understand context and vocabulary (diagnostic assessment). Through the visit the teacher may identify students' knowledge and understanding of the content, determine whether the students can construct meaning from visual art and assess the students' vocabulary and knowledge of the subject. This also enables the teacher to adapt further teaching to the needs of the students.

Formats of assessment:
The formats of assessment are diverse: from analysis of content to a research project or a debate. The judgement of student learning includes mainly written, oral and visual formats. By using formative and integrative assessments, the teacher prepares the students for the final summa-

tive assessment but also uses the assessments as a teaching and learning tool to identify the stages of student learning and clarify student understanding.
To prepare students for the summative assessment, constructive feedback is provided promptly in the form of individual and group feedback. This is achieved via written comments by the teacher and by peers for each student's work. In addition, a general discussion in the class allows students to engage with the feedback and evaluate the tasks through critical dialogue and/or peer review; this procedure encourages both self and peer assessment and development.

Formative and summative assessment:
The teacher uses a criterion-based reference system in relation to formative assessment tasks. When no marks are awarded in formative assessment, competency gradations (i.e. highly competent, competent, not yet competent) are utilised as a guide to determine the students' levels of understanding. Both the students and the teacher use the informal results internally to highlight areas of strengths or weaknesses; any examples of weaknesses would, of course, require focused improvement. In this example, most assessment tasks are both formative and summative. Thus, they require a judgement, and a mark is attached to every activity that is assessed. A final test takes place at the end of the term but only contributes 25% to the final grade.

Feedback:
The teacher ensures that individual feedback as written comments and/or group feedback discussions in class are prompt and detailed. She uses a language that clarifies concepts to create understanding and is always kind and constructive with her criticism. In order for feedback to foster self-regulated learning, she uses the students' responses to her constructive feedback to stimulate dialogue, engagement and critique through peer review, thereby allowing them to participate in discussion, set goals and play an active role in assessment and feedback.

Rubric:
In formative assessment, the rubric is an indicator for student development throughout a project or term; it encourages the students to take responsibility for their learning by allowing them to facilitate and observe their progress. In this case, the teacher created a rubric to assess the portfolio.

Lastly, the assessment of the teacher's teaching by the students is essential, as it provides valuable insight into students' thoughts on the effectiveness of his/her teaching, learning and assessment practices.

4.10 Concluding remarks: a compulsory check-list of ten principles for assessors

For an assessment to be effective, alignment between the learning objectives of a module or course – i.e. the skills, competences and knowledge that students are expected to acquire – and the teaching, learning and assessment methods chosen is crucial. Aligning them will not only benefit the students by ensuring the validity, reliability and transparency of the assessments but can help to ensure that the 'right' skills and knowledge are being assessed at the right time using appropriate methods. Below you find some ideas that support you in this process (Brown, 2001; Zimmermann, 2014):

1. What values underlie your approach to assessment in higher education? How are they manifested in practice? Is assessment designed so that students focus on acquiring the desired competences? Is assessment for learning placed at the centre of the subject and programme design? Is your assessment inclusive?
2. What intended learning objectives do you assess? How well is your approach to assessment aligned with these outcomes? Do they aim for higher levels of the cognitive domain (e.g. from Bloom's taxonomy)?

3. How do you justify your choice of assessment methods, formats and tasks used to assess the objectives in question 2? When appropriate, refer to relevant research on assessment in your answer.
4. What criteria do you base your assessment upon? Are the criteria made transparent at an early stage of the learning process? Are these criteria discussed with students?
5. Describe, justify and criticise methods of giving feedback, grading and/or marking. How do you ascertain the validity of your assessment? How do you account for avoidance of cognitive bias?
6. Describe, justify and criticise your marking techniques to overcome the following:
   i. variations in standards on a single occasion,
   ii. variations in standards on different occasions and
   iii. variations between assessors.
7. Outline and justify your approach to providing feedback to students. Is feedback used to actively improve students' learning? Does it facilitate a positive attitude to future learning? When feedback is given, how do you make sure students act upon it?
8. Do students progressively take responsibility for assessment and feedback processes? How do students demonstrate their ability to judge the quality of their work and the work of others against agreed standards?
9. Analyse your assessment: Did it work as intended? Was it too easy or too difficult? Are there questions/assignments that were misunderstood? Were there any peculiarities? Is it valid overall?
10. Further course of action: How do you want to discuss the assessment with the students: with each student individually, in groups or in class? Are there topics/learning outcomes that will have to be addressed again?

4.11 Literature

Biggs, J. (2003). Teaching for quality learning at university. Buckingham: SHRE and Open University Press.

Boud, D., & Associates (2010). Assessment 2020: Seven propositions for assessment reform in higher education. Sydney: Australian Learning and Teaching Council. URL. www.assessmentfutures.com.

Brown, G. (2001). Assessment: A Guide for lecturers. LTSN Generic Centre Assessment Series No.3. York: Learning & Teaching Support Network.

Brown, G., Bull, J., & Pendlebury, M. (1997). Assessing student learning in higher education. London & New York: Routledge.

De Grez, L., Valcke, M. & Roozen, I. (2012), How effective are self- and peer assessment of oral presentation skills compared with teachers' assessments? Active Learning in Higher Education, 13, pp. 129-142. Online (9.10.2017): http://dx.doi.org/10.1177/1469787412441284

Earl, L. & Katz, M. (2006). Rethinking classroom assessment with purpose in mind: Assessment for, as and of Learning. Manitoba Education, Online (15.8.2017): http:// www.edu.gov.mb.ca/k12/assess/wncp/full_doc.pdf.

Eberly Center (2008/2015). Why should assessments, learning objectives, and instructional strategies be aligned? Online (15.8.2017): https://www.cmu.edu/teaching/assessment/basics/alignment.html.

ETH Zurich, Educational Development and Technology (2013). Guidelines on Grading Written Examinations. Edited by Tobias Halbherr and Claudia Schlienger. Zurich. Online (12.8.2017): https://www.ethz.ch/content/dam/ethz/special-interest/gess/department-dam/D-GESS%20DAM%20General/Dokumente/Personelles/Guidelines_GradingEN_2013_11.pdf.

Feixas, M. & Zellweger, F. (2018). Planning for impact: Individual and organizational factors influencing impact of further education. In Tobias Zimmermann, Geri Thomann and Denise Da Rin (Eds.). Weiterbildung an Hochschulen. Über Kurse und Lehrgänge hinaus. Bern: Hep.

Gaston, P. (2011). Rubric used for grading an analytical essay (Sociology). Berkeley: University of California, Berkeley. Online (29.8.2017): http://

teaching.berkeley.edu/sites/default/files/general/ sociologyrubric_gradinganalyticalessay.pdf
Gibbs, G. & Simpson, C. (2004). Conditions under which assessment supports students' learning. Learning and Teaching in Higher Education, 1, pp. 3–31.
Greve, W. & Wentura, D. (1997). Wissenschaftliche Beobachtung. Eine Einführung. Psychologie Verlags Union, München.
Hattie, J. (2009). Visible Learning. A Synthesis of over 800 Meta-Analyses Relating to Achievement. London & New York: Routledge.
Healey, M., Bradley, A., Fuller, M. & Hall, T. (2006). Listening to students: the experiences of disabled students of learning at university. In: Adams, M. & Brown, S. (eds.). Towards inclusive learning in higher education: developing curricula for disabled students. London: Routledge.
Hilbert, M. (2012). Toward a synthesis of cognitive biases: how noisy information processing can bias human decision making. Psychological bulletin 138 (2), pp. 211–237.
Hockings, C. (2010). Inclusive learning and teaching in higher education: a synthesis of research Evidencenet. Higher Education Academy.
Hounsell, D. (2003). Student feedback, Learning and Development. M. Slowey, and D. Watson (Eds.) (pp. 67-78). SRHE & Open University Press.
Hounsell, D. (2008). Evaluating courses and teaching. H. Fry, S. Ketteridge, and S. Marshall. A handbook for teaching and learning in higher education: enhancing academic practice (pp. 198-211). Abingdon: Routledge.
Huba, M.A. & Freed, J.E. (2000). Learning-centered assessment in the college campus. Shifting the focus from teaching to learning. Boston: Allyn and Bacon.
Iller, C. & Wick, A. (2009). Prüfungen als Evaluation der Kompetenzentwicklung im Studium. Das Hochschulwesen, 57, 6, pp. 195–201.
Ingenkamp, K. & Lissmann, U. (2008). Lehrbuch der Pädagogischen Diagnostik. 6th edition. Weinheim, Basel: Beltz.
Ion, G., Barrera, A. & Tomas, M. (2016). Written peer-feedback to enhance students'current and future learning. International Journal of Educational Technology in Higher Education, 13(15), pp. 1–11.

Metzger, C. & Nüesch, C. (2004). Fair prüfen: Ein Qualitätsleitfaden für Prüfende an Hochschulen. St. Gallen: Universität St. Gallen, Institut für Wirtschaftspädagogik.

Plymouth University (2014). 7 Steps to: Inclusive Assessment. Online (12.7.2017): https://www.plymouth.ac.uk/uploads/production/document/path/2/2401/7_Steps_to_Inclusive_Assessment.pdf.

Sacher, W. (2014). Leistungen entwickeln, überprüfen und beurteilen. Bewährte und neue Wege für die Primar- und Sekundarstufe. 6th revised and amended edition. Bad Heilbrunn: Klinkhardt.

Sadler, D.R. (2013) Assuring academic achievement standards: from moderation to calibration. Assessment in Education: Principles, Policy & Practice, 20 (1), pp. 5-19.

Sluijsmans, D., Prins, F. J. & Martens, R. L. (2006). The Design of Competency-Based Performance Assessment in E-Learning. Learning Environments Research, 9, pp. 45–66.

UNESCO (1994). The Salamanca Statement and Framework for Action on Special Needs Education. (Online 13.7.2017): http://www.unesco.org/education/pdf/SALAMA_E.PDF.

Wieman, C.E.; Rieger, G.W. & Heiner, C. E. (2018). Physics exams that promote collaborative learning. (Online 2.3.2018): http://www.cwsei.ubc.ca/SEI_research/files/Physics/Wieman-Rieger-Heiner_Two-Stage-Exam_PT2014.pdf

Winter, F. (2012). Leistungsbewertung. Eine neue Lernkultur braucht einen anderen Umgang mit den Schülerleistungen. 5th revised and amended edition. Baltmannsweiler: Schneider Verlag Hohengehren.

Zimmermann, T. (2014). Durchführen von lernzielorientierten Leistungsnachweisen. In: Bachmann, H. (Ed.), Kompetenzorientierte Hochschullehre: Die Notwendigkeit von Kohärenz zwischen Lernzielen, Prüfungsformen und Lehr-Lern-Methoden. Bern: Hep.

Ulrike Hanke

5 Evidence-based teaching – lessons you can learn from psychology for your teaching practice

Although it is quite difficult to define what teaching is and what it is not (Hanke 2012), the first chapters of this book have already drawn attention to a commonly held consensus, namely that teaching is supposed to help someone learn (Collins 2018). For this reason, teaching should always be based on considerations about learning (Bachmann 2003, Hanke 2008, Hanke & Winandy 2014). How is information stored in the brain? Which cognitive processes take place while learning? How is information processed? How are information and new skills integrated in a sustainable manner into an individual's knowledge and cognitive structure? And last but not the least, how are these skills and information recalled? The answers to these questions are the basis for a student-centred teaching strategy, i.e. to teach in such a way that it helps students learn.

MOMBI 2.0 is an attempt to create a teaching strategy systematically, using findings from the learning sciences and neuroscience. MOMBI is an acronym for **M**odel **O**f **M**odel-**B**ased **I**nstruction. MOMBI 2.0 is an updated version of MOMBI that Hanke developed in 2008. This chapter presents MOMBI 2.0 as a student-oriented teaching strategy that takes the shift from teaching to learning seriously (see Chapter 1).

In a first step, this chapter describes the fundamentals of MOMBI 2.0 according to findings from cognitive psychology and learning sciences, together with relevant results from the neurosciences concerning the role of motivation and emotions. Then, the consequences of these considerations are discussed and synthesised in MOMBI 2.0. In addition, specific teaching methods and tools will be explained in terms of their practical application, thereby enabling teachers to use MOMBI in their classes.

5.1 Learning and its conditions

The idea of MOMBI 2.0 is to use knowledge about learning to come up with clear suggestions for teaching. The basic assumption of MOMBI 2.0 is that learning is a process of constructing new knowledge and skills in a highly individual manner; this ideally occurs in a relaxed and positive environment. The process of learning can be described in more detail as six subprocesses. In order to implement a relaxed and positive learning environment, the need for autonomy, social relatedness and competence also have to be satisfied. For an overview, see Figure 1. This model will be elaborated in subsequent sections of this chapter.

Figure 1 Subprocesses of learning in a positive learning environment.

According to Piaget (1976), learning is provoked by a mental disequilibrium, i.e. situations that individuals encounter as puzzling or inexplicable **(subprocess 1: provocation of mental disequilibrium)**. The provocation can be one or all of the following:

- questions that learners cannot answer and/or
- statements or information that they do not understand and/or
- visual, auditory or even tactile perceptions that irritate them.

Curiosity, therefore, causes people to learn, because curiosity is the natural and innate motor of learning (Kang et al. 2009, Jäncke 2013).

A study by Kang et al. (2009) showed that asking students questions at the beginning of a lesson attracted their attention and supported learning new content in an effective way. Evidently, these questions stimulated their curiosity and, in order to satisfy that curiosity, they were willing to make the necessary effort to learn because they had a goal: they wanted to find out the answers.

Since human beings prefer to be in a state of equilibrium, a disequilibrium causes discomfort and leads to mental activation (Seel 1991, Wittrock 1990); individuals begin to think about what they have perceived and what possible answers or reactions would be helpful in this situation. In this way, individuals activate – quasi automatically – their prior knowledge to re-establish their mental equilibrium **(subprocess 2: activation of prior knowledge)**. Re-establishing the equilibrium is the goal that drives them **(subprocess 3: goal setting)**.

When they do not come up with a plausible answer or solution, human beings start searching for the missing information (Dreistadt 1969, Seel 1991). They ask someone, they search for information on the internet or read a book, etc. **(subprocess 4: search for information)**.

While searching, they try to integrate the new information into their existing cognitive structure and stop searching when this integration process is successful (Seel 1991), i.e. when the state of equilibrium has been re-established. This is the moment when they have the impression that they have found the answer or solution or that they can explain the formerly irritating situation **(subprocess 5: integration)**.

If individuals value the new information or if the new information touches them emotionally, they will elaborate on it (Wellenreuther 2012, Hattie 2013). This means that they will think or talk about it, they will do further exercises or memorise it, i.e. they will stay busy with the new information or skill **(subprocess 6: elaboration)**. This is why emotionally enriched information is remembered more easily.

Summing up, the underlying assumptions of MOMBI 2.0 are:

- Learning is provoked by an irritating situation, which puts individuals in a state of mental disequilibrium.
- In order to re-establish their mental equilibrium, individuals begin to activate their prior knowledge, because they have set a goal to re-establish their mental equilibrium.
- If their existing knowledge is not sufficient, they begin to search for the missing information and carry on searching until they are able to integrate the new information into their existing structure. This is the moment of the purported click of comprehension.
- If the new information seems important to the individuals, they begin to elaborate on it to retain it – and never forget or unlearn it.

After individuals have successfully passed through all these subprocesses, they have changed their cognitive structures. Learning has taken place.

Learning processes in the manner described above are hampered in emotionally negative contexts. There is evidence that learning is more successful in emotionally positive learning environments. Negative feelings, such as anxiety or fear, inhibit learning (Shakman et al. 2006), because – innately – human reactions to fear are fight or flight. Although human beings have the capacity to react in various ways, fear puts them under stress; the first thing they do in a stressful situation is to find ways to reduce that stress. This search for stress reduction calls up all the cognitive capacities, which means that there are hardly any capacities left for elaborating on academic content. Human beings in a state of fear automatically direct their attention to the source of the fear and not to the academic content that should be learned. Therefore, it is important to create learning situations that promote positive emotions. Students need learning environments in which they feel free to think and learn, in which they are confident that they are respected – even if they make mistakes – and in which they can use all their cognitive capacities to engage in learning. Myths such as "learning takes place best under pressure" or "students are supposed to fear teachers – if they don't, they won't respect the teachers" are nonsense (for a deconstruction of this myth, see Ulrich 2016).

However, what are the characteristics of positive learning environments? Pondering on this question, it is helpful to consider the self-determination theory of Deci and Ryan (1993). This theory assumes that – when primary and secondary needs, such as the need for food and shelter, are satisfied – individuals have three basic needs: the need for autonomy, the need for social relatedness and the need for competence. When these three needs are satisfied, individuals feel good and motivated. For this reason, teachers should make sure to satisfy these needs of their students during the entire teaching process. Self-directed learning, collaborative learning arrangements and competence orientation are decisive in satisfying these needs.

Another important finding to consider for teaching is that individuals remember highly emotional content better than neutrally-presented information (Jäncke 2013, 2014), because the emotional aspects represent something with which the new information can be connected. The more connections a knowledge chunk has in the cognitive and neuronal structure, the easier it is to activate this structure or chunk later on (Beck 2015, Jäncke 2014).

5.2 Consequences for teaching

Considering the six steps of the learning process, six complementary teaching interventions are suggested (see MOMBI 2.0 in Figure 2). Each of these teaching interventions is supposed to provoke or support precisely one of the subprocesses of learning. In addition, MOMBI 2.0 integrates – as a basis for positive and motivating learning environments – the three environmental aspects associated with the three needs that have to be satisfied.

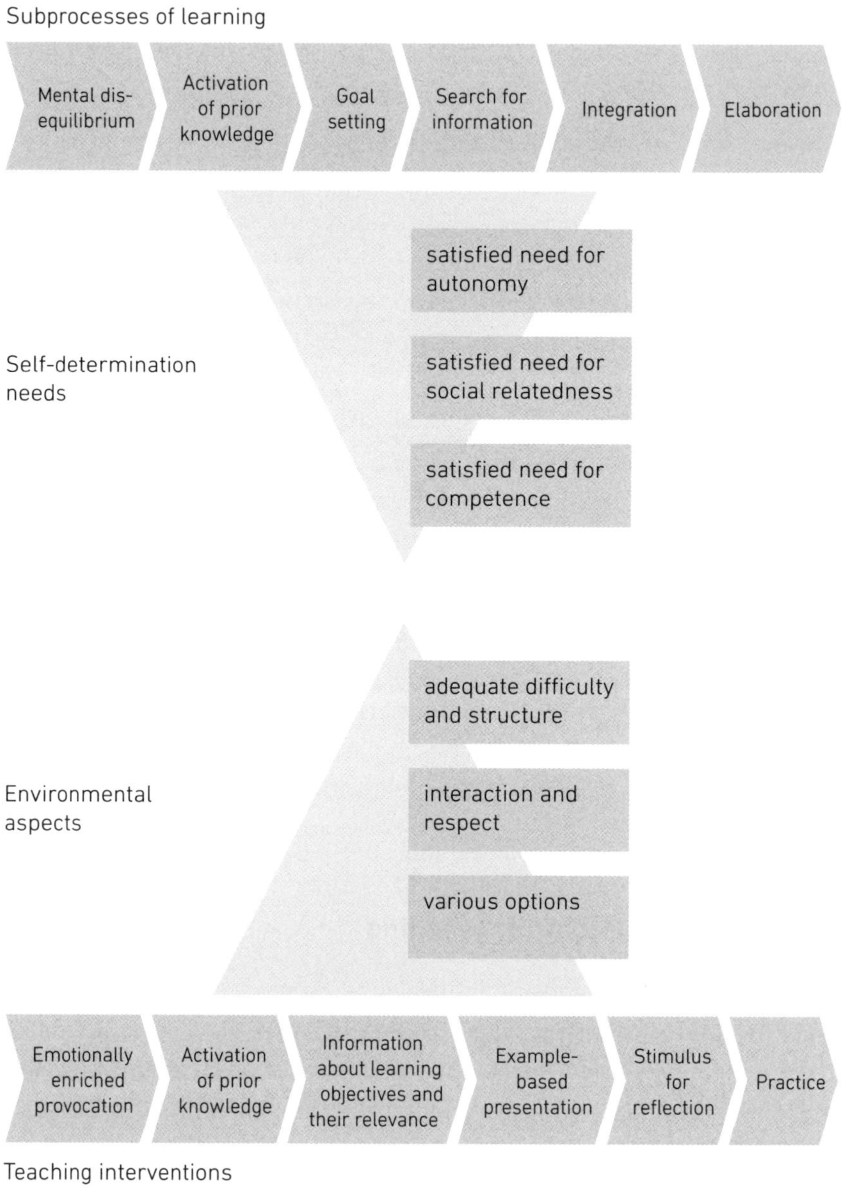

Figure 2 Model of model-base instruction.

The next sections of this chapter present the six teaching interventions, together with methods and tools for their implementation. This is followed by an explanation of the three environmental aspects, an elaboration of various ideas associated with them and a description of how these environmental aspects can be met.

5.2.1 Teaching interventions

In the following sections, the six teaching interventions of MOMBI 2.0 are presented, and examples of tools and methods are explained. Figure 3 summarises possible teaching methods for each intervention.

5.2.2 Teaching intervention: emotionally enriched provocation

Since learning is provoked by a mental disequilibrium, MOMBI 2.0 suggests (see Figure 2) that teaching should begin with such a provoked mental disequilibrium (**teaching intervention 1: emotionally enriched provocation**). This provocation attracts the learners' attention.

This can be done by piquing the students' curiosity regarding the learning content. In natural learning contexts, e.g. when very young children learn, it is their curiosity that drives them. Teachers should therefore use this opportunity and make their students curious about the learning content. This activates their relevant neuronal structures.

Since human beings memorise better when learning content is presented in an emotional way, using provocations that touch the students emotionally can support learning.

- Teachers can, for example, present facts from the learning content that the students find new and surprising or that irritate them and make them curious,
- They can use videos, headlines, pictures/graphics/comics, statements or questions,

- They can also present problems or case studies or tell students a story about themselves or another person with whom the students can somehow identify.

In this way, teachers motivate the students to start working on authentic tasks, which is one of the dimensions of excellent teaching and learning in higher education (see Chapter 1, Figure 11). Teachers can use anything that attracts their students' attention and touches them emotionally. However, teachers have to be careful not to trigger anxiety or fear in students. Anxiety and fear also trigger a mental disequilibrium – but this disequilibrium provokes stress reduction activities and not the elaboration of cognitive learning strategies.

5.2.3 Teaching intervention: activation of prior knowledge

Since the activation of prior knowledge is important for learning, MOMBI 2.0 recommends that the students are asked – as the second teaching intervention – to activate their prior knowledge as regards the provocation **(teaching intervention 2: activation of prior knowledge)**.

This teaching intervention can be implemented by asking the students to react and respond to the provocation with which they were confronted in the first teaching intervention. The teaching interventions "Provocation" and "Activation of prior knowledge" are therefore extremely interrelated. There is no need for a new question or anything else to that effect. Teachers can use the fact/content of the provocation.

But teachers can ask the students – in different ways – to react to the provocation. It is possible to

- ask the entire group and wait for answers,
- ask the students to discuss their reactions and answers in buzz groups for two to three minutes; this is much more stimulating and less-threatening for the majority of students than asking the entire group of students,
- ask the students to design a mind or concept map,

- ask the students to brainstorm,
- ask the students to arrange small cards with concepts or questions in a reasonable way and to explain the concepts or answer the questions that are written on the cards (Macke et al. 2016). This activity requires the teacher to prepare the cards in advance.

Taking the processes of learning into account, this activation of prior knowledge is important. However, it can be quite frustrating when the students believe that they do not have sufficient knowledge to re-establish mental equilibrium. For this reason, it is important that the teaching intervention "Activation of prior knowledge" is followed by the teaching intervention "Information about learning objectives and their relevance".

5.2.4 Teaching intervention: information about learning objectives and their relevance

In order to avoid frustrations as a result of the triggered disequilibrium, it is important to present learning objectives to the students at this stage of the lesson. It is also important, to explain their relevance in order to re-establish an equilibrium **(teaching intervention 3: information about learning objectives and their relevance)**. When students understand the relevance of the learning objectives, they have a reason to pay attention during the lesson (see also Chapter 1, Figure 11).

There are not many alternatives for implementing this teaching intervention, but in order to strengthen the students' motivation, as well as constructive alignment, it is a very important teaching intervention. Students need to understand how the design of the lesson, the intended learning objectives and the assessment are interrelated. For this reason, teachers need to explain to their students (a) what they can learn in the lesson and (b) what the relevance of the content and the objectives is. In order to ensure that the students understand the relevance of the learning objectives, it is important to use their language when describing the objectives (Arn 2016). An overly technical description will not convince the students that the objectives are worth pursuing.

5.2.5 Teaching intervention: example-based presentation

In order to help students find the information needed to re-establish mental equilibrium, the presentation of information is the fourth teaching intervention **(teaching intervention 4: example-based presentation)**.

Other than using a traditional presentation to implement this teaching intervention, the teacher can present any form of media that contains the information the students need for re-establishing their mental equilibrium, for example:

- texts,
- videos,
- webpages,
- other experts, etc.

Regardless of which media the teachers use, they need to ensure that they give the students sufficient examples and learning content that triggers emotions, because emotionally enriched content is better remembered than neutrally presented information (Jäncke 2013, 2014).

5.2.6 Teaching intervention: stimulus for reflection

In order to actually re-establish equilibrium, it is not sufficient that students hear or read information. They also need to be supported in integrating the new information into their existing cognitive/neuronal structure. For this reason, it is important to give them stimuli for reflection and ask them to actively grapple with the new information. At this stage in the teaching and learning process, teachers can ask their students to work on authentic tasks either individually or in groups (see also Chapter 1, Figure 11, "initiate group activities"). Examples of activating teaching and learning methods include:

- asking the students to talk about the new information,
- asking them to write it down,
- asking them to apply it,

- asking them to link it to their own experiences or to examples,
- asking them to work on new tasks, problems or cases.

Figure 3 contains more examples of specific teaching methods for this intervention.

This teaching intervention **(teaching intervention 4: stimulus for reflection)** gives teachers an insight into what the students have learned and understood. As a type of assessment, this helps teachers to support their students in their individual learning processes (cf. Chapter 1, Figure 11).

5.2.7 Teaching intervention: practice

In order to ensure that the new information or skill will be available for a longer time, it is important to ask the students to practice **(teaching intervention 6: practice)**. For example, teachers should encourage students to go more into detail by giving them further exercises and tasks. In the daily practice of university teaching, the standard procedure is to ask the students to practice during self-study time. If, however, teachers have time for this teaching intervention during a lesson, they can use any teaching method to actively engage the students in reflecting about the subject in question. For this reason, adequate teaching methods for this teaching intervention are more or less similar to teaching intervention 5: stimulus for reflection.

Figure 3 lists specific teaching methods for the six teaching interventions.

Teaching intervention	Teaching methods
Emotionally enriched provocation	• Corner method[2] • Headline • Interview • Picture, graphic, comic • Question • Statement • Video
Activation of prior knowledge	• Brainstorming[2] • Buzz groups[1,2,3] • Concept mapping[2] • Group work[2] • Mind mapping[2] • Sorting task[2] • Think-pair-share[1,2]
Presentation of learning objectives and their relevance	• Present the intended learning objectives in relation to the lesson and assessment • Use students' language • Explain the relevance of reaching the objectives for the students (in their life)
Example-based presentation	• Interview[2] • Presentation, speech • Text • Video • Webpages and links on internet
Stimulus for reflection	• Analytic teams[1] • Buzz groups[1,2,3] • Critical debate[1] • Group work[2] • Note-taking-pairs[1,2,3] • Reframing[3] • Send-a-problem[1,2,3] • Sequence chains[1] • Think-pair-share[1,2] • Word webs[1]
Practice	• Homework • Individual work • Transfer tasks

Figure 3 Teaching methods for the teaching interventions of MOMBI 2.0 ([1] Barkley et al. 2005, [2] Macke et al. 2016, [3] Hanke 2018).

5.2.8 Considering emotions in teaching – environmental aspects

As already discussed, learning occurs best in non-fearful situations. Therefore, teachers have to create a positive learning environment in which students feel comfortable and are able to concentrate on learning. As already described, students experience learning environments in positive ways when their needs for autonomy, social relatedness and competence are satisfied.

5.2.9 Various options

In order to ensure student autonomy, it is helpful when teachers offer their students "various options". This can be done by implementing teaching methods that allow students to choose and/or individualise the learning process. Methods that allow for choices are the following:

- Students select a topic for their presentation (e.g. from a predefined selection by the teacher),
- Students choose their partners when they have to work in pairs or groups,
- Students decide if they want to work alone or in pairs,
- Students choose the topic they would like to work on,
- Students can determine their own learning pace as often as possible.

The "learning stations" method (Macke et al. 2016) is very effective at offering students a variety of different possibilities to make their own decisions. In order to implement this method, teachers prepare different "learning stations". A learning station consists of information for the students to work with, e.g. texts, videos, links etc., together with an accompanying task to expand the information. Teachers can also use assignments that are similar to exam questions. This helps the students assess their own strengths and weaknesses, and the teachers can help them to "overcome learning obstacles", as mentioned in Figure 11 in Chapter 1.

During the lesson, the students are asked to move from one station to the next, solving the tasks. The students are allowed to work at their own pace, which is a big advantage of this method. They can also choose the tasks that are most relevant to them in order to reach the learning objectives. In this setting, the teacher can act as a coach and support students individually.

The challenge of this teaching method is the task preparation. This is quite time consuming. However, as soon as the tasks are prepared, they can easily be reused in other teaching contexts.

In addition to the "learning stations" teaching method, any method that enables the students to work on their own gives them autonomy. Standard teacher presentations, however, limit the students' autonomy significantly.

5.2.10 Respect and interaction

In order to satisfy the need for social relatedness, it is important to give students opportunities to interact with each other and their teachers.

All types of group work help support interaction between the students (see Chapter 1, Figure 11 "stimulating group work"). Teachers need to ensure that students do not feel isolated – even in a very large class. Teachers should always give students an opportunity to talk in class. Even if not every student appreciates this, it signals that the teachers are interested in what the students have to say.

For example, the teachers can ask the students to discuss the key messages of a specific lecture in pairs and write them down within a short period of time (e.g. between 2 and 10 minutes). The teachers can also ask their learners to define or structure the presented concepts in pairs. These exchanges, whereby students discuss questions or tasks in a short period of time with a partner, are called buzz groups.

When students have prepared texts or the teachers have just demonstrated a specific skill, the students can be asked to apply the insights they gained in problem-solving or group discussions.

These ways of stimulating students enable them to talk and communicate so that they feel socially related.

Furthermore, when teachers show interest in their work while they are working in pairs or groups, and when teachers become involved in their discussions, the effect of feeling socially related will be even more significant.

Another way in which teachers can satisfy the students' need for social relatedness is to extend opportunities for interactions between the teachers and the students, as well as between the students themselves. For example,

- the teacher can enter the classroom a few minutes before the lesson begins. This shows the students that the teacher is prepared and that the teacher is really interested in teaching them. It is a sign of respect,
- the teacher can use the time before the lesson begins to engage in small talk with the students; the teacher can also give them an opportunity to talk to him/her,
- the teacher can also invite the students to ask questions not only during class time but also before and after the lesson,
- the teacher can also explicitly communicate his/her office hours and contact information to the students. This is another indicator that makes the students feel the teacher is interested in them and also in their learning.

Another suggestion is to ask the students for honest feedback and to take their feedback seriously. This does not mean that teachers should implement everything that their students demand; but when students give feedback, the teachers should justify why they cannot always comply with the students' requests. Teachers should make a point of having good debates when students' ideas are turned down. Studies show that regular feedback in both directions results in better learning (Schneider & Preckel 2017).

Teachers could also use the "smiley face method" to generate students' feedback. After about one third of the semester, teachers could ask their students at the end of a class to draw a happy smiley face and a sad smiley face on a piece of paper and to add comments – under the smiley faces – about what they have liked and disliked about the classes up to now. The teachers then collect these papers and read their students' comments. In this way, teachers will sense how to proceed with their courses.

By asking for feedback and taking it seriously, the teachers show "respect". This is very important for creating a positive learning environment.

5.2.11 Adequate difficulty and structure

In order to satisfy the need for competence, it is important that the structure of the lesson is both adequately difficult and transparent.

Regarding the entire design of the lesson, teachers must ensure that their students are challenged but able to cope. The students must be given tasks and exercises that are manageable but at the same time challenging. Such an approach promotes feelings of success.

In order to create adequate tasks and exercises, it is very important to obtain as much information as possible about the background of the students. Teachers must make sure that they know what the students are supposed to know. The teachers must also know which skills the students are supposed to have. In this way, the teachers can adapt their lesson designs to the students' needs and skills.

Furthermore, the students should be given individual tasks and receive individual feedback. Teachers should help them recognise their personal progress, their strengths and weaknesses and reflect with them about their individual professional development (see Chapter 1, Figure 11 "reflecting learning processes").

Teachers can also satisfy the need for competence by orienting the students about the semester programme and the individual classes. A written plan of the class, to which the teacher refers from time to time, can be helpful because it "structures" the session. If teachers refer to this plan after every major step in a class and show the students which aspects have already been dealt with, the students are able to see their progress more clearly.

Evidently, there are a variety of possibilities that help implement a positive learning environment. Although teachers will not be able to implement all of them at the same time, they should consider at least a few of them in every lesson.

5.3 Summary

All in all, when teachers consider the environmental aspects and implement all six teaching interventions mentioned in this chapter, their students will learn more effectively and their success will last longer. MOMBI 2.0 can therefore be very helpful for focussing on those aspects in the learning environment that are important when designing learning arrangements that promote learning. Despite the function of MOMBI 2.0 to structure the learning process, it is, nevertheless, a flexible strategy: teachers always have various choices as to how to implement the teaching interventions and how to include the relevant environmental aspects. It is not rigid, and lessons can be conducted in very different ways.

Since MOMBI 2.0 is based on research findings about learning, it meets all the dimensions of excellent teaching and learning in higher education, which Bachmann recommends in Chapter 1, Figure 11. Lessons that are created by taking MOMBI 2.0 into consideration are thereby student-centred and learning-oriented.

5.4 Literature

Arn, C. (2016). Agile Hochschuldidaktik. Weinheim: Beltz.

Bachmann, H. (2003). Auch Lernen will gelernt sein. Aarau: Sauerländer.

Barkley, E. F., Cross, K. P., & Major, C. H. (2005). Collaborative Learning Techniques. San Francisco: Jossey-Bass.

Beck, H. (2015). Hirnrissig. Die 20,5 größten Neuromythen – und wie unser Gehirn wirklich tickt. Munich: Goldmann-Verlag.

Collins English Dictionary (2018), abrufbar unter: https://www.collinsdictionary.com/dictionary/english. Online (24.3.2018)

Deci, Edward L. & Ryan, Richard M. (1993). Die Selbstbestimmungstheorie der Motivation und ihre Bedeutung für die Pädagogik. In: Zeitschrift für Pädagogik 39, pp. 223-238.

Dreistadt, R. (1969). The use of analogies and incubation in obtaining insights in creative problem solving. Journal of Psychology, 71, pp. 159-175.

Hanke, U. (2008). Realizing model-based instruction. The model of model-based instruction. In: Ifenthaler, D., Spector, M. & Pirnay-Dummer, P (Eds.), Understanding Models for Learning and Instruction. Essays in Honor of Norbert M. Seel (pp. 175-186). New York: Springer.

Hanke, U. (2012). Bedingungen und Prozesse des Lehrens. Warum Lehrende unterrichten, wie sie unterrichten. Saarbrücken: SVH Südwestdeutscher Verlag für Hochschulschriften.

Hanke, U. (2018). Methoden-Schatzkiste. Online (7.6.2018): https://www.hanke-teachertraining.de/didaktik-schatzkiste/lehrmethoden-schatzkiste/

Hanke, U. & Winandy, S. (ed.) (2014). Lernförderlich Lehren. Tübinger Beiträge zur Hochschuldidaktik 10/2. Online (9.06.2018): http://hdl.handle.net/10900/53782

Hattie, J. (2013). Lernen sichtbar machen. Baltmannweiler: Schneider-Verlag Hohengehren.

Jäncke, L. (2013). Kognitive Neurowissenschaften. Bern: Huber.

Jäncke, L. (2014). Die Neurobiologie des menschlichen Lernens. In: Bachmann, H. (ed.), Kompetenzorientierte Hochschullehre. Die Notwendigkeit

von Kohärenz zwischen Lernzielen, Prüfungsformen und Lehr-Lern-Methoden (pp. 127-146). 2nd revised and amended edition. Bern: hep.
Kang, M. J., Hsu, M., Krajbich, T.M., Loewenstein, C., McClure, S.M., Wang, J. T., & Camerer, C.F. (2009). The Wick in the Candle of Learning. Psychological Science, 20 (8), 963-973.
Macke, G., Hanke, U., Viehmann, P. & Raether, W. (2016). Kompetenzorientierte Hochschuldidaktik. Lehren, Vortragen, Prüfen, Beraten. 3rd revised edition. Weinheim: Beltz.
Piaget, J. (1976). Die Äquilibration der kognitiven Strukturen. Stuttgart: Klett Verlag
Schneider, M. & Preckel, F. (2017). Variables Associated With Achievement in Higher Education: A Systematic Review of Meta-Analysis. Psychological Bulletin. Online (2.02.2018): http://dx.doi.org/10.1037/bul0000098.
Seel, N. M. (1991). Weltwissen und mentale Modelle. Göttingen u.a.: Hogrefe.
Shackman A.J., Sarinopoulos I., Maxwell J.S., Pizzagalli D.A., Lavric A. & Davidson R.J. (2006). Anxiety selectively disrupts visuospatial working memory. Emotion, 6 (1), pp. 40-61.
Ulrich, I. (2016). Gute Lehre in der Hochschullehre. Praxistipps zur Planung und Gestaltung von Lehrveranstaltungen. Wiesbaden: Springer.
Wellenreuther, M. (2012). Forschungsbasierte Schulpädagogik. Baltmannsweiler: Schneider Verlag Hohengehren.
Wittrock, M. C. (1990). Generative Processes of Comprehension. Educational Psychologist, 24, pp. 345-376.

Glossary

Action-oriented teaching

Such teaching is based on a holistic learning process in which students actively participate with other students to solve a problem using their knowledge and skills. In action-oriented teaching environments, four principles need to be considered:

- **The principle of self-motivated learning and student engagement** which, among other things, refers to the students' autonomy in designing their own activities.
- **The principle of being student-oriented** which, among other things, means building on the students' prior knowledge and expertise and also on orienting the teaching towards sparking their interest (e.g. "awakening curiosity").
- **The principle of being true-to-life** which refers to a reality orientation. The central idea is that reasoning develops from practical actions in real-life situations.
- **The principle of wholeness and meaning** which, among other things, refers to enabling complete action sequences, the systemic investigation of how things are related and the integration of cognitive, affective and psychomotor processes in learning.

Assessment

Evaluation process that gives an indication on students' learning. As a qualification instrument it forms the basis for selection. A distinction is made between two fundamentally different assessment purposes:

- **Formative** assessment is primarily used to monitor learning progress and serves to optimise student learning by giving feedback.
- **Summative** assessment refers to the process of testing for selection purposes. It measures to what extent the learner has achieved the pre-defined learning outcomes.

Assessment and observation errors

Interpretive distortions that occur when performance can only be assessed indirectly via students' written or oral statements. These interpretations are subject to distortions.

Assessment reference standard

See benchmark

Benchmark

The norm against which measurements are made in performance evaluation. To make a statement about performance quality, one has to objectively consider the difficulties associated with a specific task as well as the student's level of education. One can distinguish between three different types of benchmark:

- **Personal** benchmark – students are measured according to their personal development.
- **Learning-outcome-oriented** benchmark – students are measured according to pre-defined learning objectives.
- **Social** benchmark – students are measured in comparison to each other, within a particular group.

Blended learning

A form of learning that combines traditional classroom teaching and modern forms of e-learning. Face-to-face communication and online activities – alone or together with peers – complement each other.

Bologna Process

A reform process in higher education across Europe, which started in 1999. The Bologna Process is driven by the ambitious vision of making Europe the most competitive, dynamic and knowledge-based economic area in the world. To achieve this, a declaration for a pan-European academic reform was written and signed in Bologna in 1999. By now, approximately 50 European states have joined this reform movement. The four cornerstones of the Bologna Process are:

- restructuring higher education degree programmes (*Bachelor/Master/Doctorate*),
- transparency, comparability and mutual recognition of requirements and standards in higher education programmes and modules across Europe (*ECTS, workload, competences*),
- quality assurance in higher education (*EQF - European Qualifications Framework / NQF - National Qualifications Framework*),
- higher education realignment to fit current and expected future developments in a globalised, knowledge-based economy (*lifelong learning, employability, mobility, digitalisation*).

Case-based learning (CBL)

Students become involved in discussions about real-world, authentic examples. They are required to collaboratively analyse and solve problems; they tackle questions that have no single right answer. CBL tends to be more highly structured and more closely guided than problem-based learning (PBL).

Closed task

See examinations and tests.

Competence

The ability to combine knowledge, skills and experience to solve real problems in seemingly puzzling and complex situations. Competences also include motivational elements such as willingness to solve a problem, the perseverance to overcome setbacks or being optimistic that a solution can be found. In addition to discipline-specific competences (expertise), interdisciplinary competences (soft skills or key/transversal competences) are becoming increasingly important. These include methodological skills (languages, learning strategies, IT, etc.), social skills (conflict management, cooperation skills, etc.) and personal skills (ethical awareness, capacity for self-criticism, etc.).

Construction

In pedagogy, this refers to learning in which students engage with the learning material relatively independently and actively. They construct meaning for themselves. A project that students do independently is an example of such constructive engagement.

Constructive alignment

The alignment of learning outcomes, teaching and learning methods and appropriate forms of assessment. Depending on the learning objectives in a given module, certain teaching and assessment formats are better than others. Social skills cannot, for example, be examined using a multiple-choice examination.

Convergent performance

See performance.

Dacum

A process for "developing a curriculum". The point of departure for dacum is an analysis of professional requirements (i.e. competences) from various perspectives, namely those of the employers, the employees and the trainees. The analysis can be subsequently used to set, design and develop a curriculum for academic institutions, especially technical colleges that prepare students for specific professions.

Design thinking

An iterative problem-solving strategy in which the data collected is expressed visually in order to create new strategies, ways and methods to solve problems and to create opportunities or strengthen weaknesses.

Divergent performance

See performance.

Deep learning

See surface learning.

Dublin Descriptors

Terms that describe the various levels of expected achievement associated with the three university degrees (Bachelor/Master/Doctorate). They are based on general learning outcomes or competences. An example of such a descriptor is: "Students are able to collect and interpret data that is relevant to their field of study and to support their findings by taking the relevant social, scientific and ethical interests into account."

ECTS

European Credit Transfer System. The European Credit Transfer System uses "credit points" as a unit to quantify student workload. One ECTS credit point equals 25 to 30 working hours. The workload calculation should incorporate self-study time, time spent in the classroom and preparation for tests or examinations. In Switzerland, financial support for universities is also calculated on the basis of ECTS points. The ECTS facilitates transfer of students between universities across Europe by making transparent the level of achievement she or he has attained; it also gives employers information about the standard a prospective employee has reached, regardless of where qualifications were acquired.

Employability

Fitness for the labour market. One of the objectives of the Bologna Process is to prepare graduates for the labour market.

EQF

European Qualifications Framework. The European Qualifications Framework for higher education provides relatively general descriptions of degree programmes in order to assure transparency and comparability across European universities. The EQF includes descriptions of the workload, standards, learning outcomes and competences. The National Qualifications Framework (NQF) specifies the more general statements of the EQF for a specific country and also regulates the transfer possibilities for students.

Examinations and tests

They are often categorised according to the following criteria:

- **Closed** tasks: closed tasks have one correct answer.
- **Semi-open** tasks: the answer is often not precisely defined, although the teachers have a clear idea of what the correct solution should be.
- **Open** tasks are not predetermined, so that the students as well as the teachers do not know in advance what kinds of answers they will ultimately accept as correct.

Explicit knowledge

Knowledge which students have and can consciously articulate if necessary.

Extrinsic motivation

External rewards for learning behaviour, such as grades, money, parental or instructor approval.

Flipped classroom

An instructional strategy that reverses traditional teaching-learning interactions, making them more learner-centred. Content is delivered via reading assignments or videos that the learner works through independently. Classroom time is dedicated to exploring the topic in greater depth, to discussions or debates, laboratory experiments, problem-solving exercises, etc. Classroom activities also foster collaborative and peer learning. The flipped classroom strategy can also incorporate blended learning or MOOCs (Massive Open Online Courses).

Formative assessment

See assessment.

Grading

One can distinguish between numerical grades and basic grades:

- **Numerical grades** are problematic in that they have several disadvantages compared to more detailed (written or oral) feedback about performance. Numerical grades suggest an exact measurability and comparability of performances, thereby presuming an unrealistic accuracy and differentiation. Such grades promote unnecessary competition between the learners, and they do not give any details about content.

- **Basic grades**, on the other hand, are an indispensable component of evaluation. This refers to roughly graded judgements such as improvement, consistent performance or deterioration (in personal benchmarking) or exceeding, meeting or failing to achieve the requirements (in learning-outcome-oriented benchmarking).

Inert knowledge

This refers to the gap between knowledge and skills. The term describes the phenomenon of people having increasingly more knowledge due to the information explosion but being so overwhelmed by the amount that they are at a loss on how to apply it appropriately.

Input orientation

An orientation to the content/material that students need to master.

Instruction

Teaching process that refers to a learning environment in which especially the omniscient teacher informs the "ignorant" students about what they have to learn and how to do so. The lecture is a classic example of this type of knowledge transfer.

Interdisciplinary competences

See competence.

Intrinsic motivation

Motivation that arises when the reward the learner gets comes from within, i.e. when his/her satisfaction comes from intensely engaging in a task. Ideally, learners will learn a subject because they are interested in it and not because of the grade.

Learner voice

In terms of being learner-oriented, Rudd, Colligan & Naik (2006) encourage teachers to enter into a dialogue with learners (listen to the learner) to better understand their perceptions, difficulties, hopes, fears, etc.

Learning

Gain or acquire knowledge or skills in a specific area by studying, experience or being taught. Learning leads to a relatively long-lasting change in a person's behaviour or in the ability to act consciously in a certain way, based on prior experience.

Learning outcomes/learning objectives *(used synonymously in this book)*

Learning outcomes are statements of what a learner knows, understands and is able to do upon completion of a learning process. The achievement of learning outcomes has to be assessed by procedures based on clear and transparent criteria. Good learning outcomes are expressed as "can do" statements.

Life-long learning

In view of rapid economic and technological changes, it is essential that professionals constantly continue to educate themselves. The Bologna Process makes provision for the equivalent recognition of formal knowledge gained in schools, vocational schools and universities, alongside knowledge acquired informally at work.

Numeric grades

See grading.

NQF

National Qualifications Framework; see the EQF.

Objectivity

See quality criteria for performance assessment.

Open task

See examinations and tests.

Output orientation
This refers to the competences students must have after completing their studies.

Peer evaluation
See self and peer assessment.

Performance
Student performance refers to the activities with which they try to achieve the educational or curricular objectives as well as the results of achieving these targets. "Performance" can therefore refer to both the process that leads to performance, as well as its results. One can distinguish between convergent and divergent performance:

- **Convergent** performance can be accurately measured on the basis of a correct or clearly best result.
- **Divergent** performance can lead to many equivalent results that cannot be compared by using only one correct way of measuring.

Personal benchmark
See benchmark.

Portfolio
Portfolios are used to document the learning process. Basically, there are three different types of portfolios:

- **Assessment portfolio**. A collection of products to evaluate a learner's performance in a given field.
- **Working/development/reflective portfolio.** Self reflections by the learner on the learning process.
- **Display or showcase portfolio.** This demonstrates exemplary work of a learner's competences and is often used when applying for a job.

Problem-based learning (PBL)
This refers to a largely self-directed learning process in which students, working in small groups accompanied by a tutor, explore, explain and solve significant problems. There are four different design principles:

- **Complex contexts and an authentic learning environment:** The students should gain experience in complex real-world situations to promote the development of not only declarative (what) but also procedural (how) and conditional (when) knowledge. Real-world problems should be the starting point of the learning process.
- **Multiple and situational contexts**: Students learn by being exposed to multiple and diverse perspectives and to diverse methods. They are confronted with various situational requirements and have to apply their knowledge in different situations and to different problems, i.e. the scope of knowledge application is not confined to a single specific context.
- **Social contexts**: Students develop by means of team learning and teamwork in cooperative learning environments. Here, communication skills are further developed; the dialogue between teachers and students also plays a crucial role.
- **Instructional contexts**: The teacher gives students appropriate support, including mutual reflection and jointly articulating learning and problem-solving processes.

Quality criteria for performance assessment

In performance assessment, three key quality criteria have to be satisfied for their results to be considered meaningful:

- **Objectivity** (independence): An assessment outcome will count as objective if the individual assessment results are obtained irrespective of the assessor.
- **Reliability** (assessment accuracy): The more accurately and reliably an assessment measures a certain feature, the higher its reliability.
- **Validity**: A performance assessment is valid if it actually measures what it is supposed to measure, and not something else.

Reduction strategies

The process of reducing content and simplifying complex concepts to make them more manageable and understandable for students in a specific module. It entails selecting appropriate material depending on the students' existing knowledge and learning abilities, and on the competences that need to be developed.

Reliability

See quality criteria for performance measurements.

Rubric

An assessment matrix that allows a differentiated description of performance quality. It includes different performance dimensions and several performance levels, both of which are comprehensively described in words.

Scaffolding

Adaptive learner support, particularly in independent individual learning or group learning situations. Instructions, mental stimulus and other kinds of support are given to bridge the gap between existing and desired knowledge, thereby enabling learners to solve a problem or complete a task.

Self and peer assessment

Students assess themselves or their fellow students (peers). In assessing both their own and others' performances, students develop an ability to assess performance appropriately. This is important for managing their on-going learning both during the degree course and their future careers.

Self-study, guided

For a long time, self-study at universities was associated almost exclusively with preparation and revision for exams. Nowadays, teachers are encouraged to guide the students' self-study activities by designing appropriate contextual conditions (e.g. setting tasks), by providing feedback as a mentor and by being available as a discussion partner.

Semi-open task

See examinations and tests.

Shift from teaching to learning

Reorientation in higher education teaching. Here, the focus is no longer on the teacher but on the student and what he or she should be able to do. In the traditional understanding of education, the teachers only considered what was necessary for them to teach well. The new student-centred approach shifts the focus of teaching efforts to optimising student-learning processes.

Simulation game

The term “serious game” is regularly used internationally. In an educational context, the term refers to simulated results of decisions by people who adopt roles and represent interests and how they impact on interventions in system dynamics and resources.

Summative assessment

See assessment.

Social benchmark

See benchmark.

Surface learning (superficial or rote learning)

A practice of learning material by heart, without understanding, applying and integrating it. The result of such learning efforts is not sustainable, because the learned material is quickly forgotten and hardly ever transferred to practice. The opposite of surface learning is deep learning.

Taxonomy of learning objectives

The classification of learning objectives according to certain criteria. Bloom’s updated taxonomy illustrates this by differentiating six cognitive levels with ascending degrees of difficulty:

1. remembering,
2. understanding,
3. applying,
4. analysing,
5. evaluating,
6. creating.

Tutoring
A teaching and learning method which fosters the exchange of active knowledge and skills in relatively small groups. Conventionally, tutors are students in more advanced semesters who support a learning group by helping them to practice and internalise the learning material from their lectures; exercise classes are often the format led by tutors.

Validity
See quality criteria for performance measurements.

Workload
See ECTS.

Appendix

Example of a module description – intercultural communication

module description	*Intercultural communication skills are regarded as key competences in the 21st century and are, therefore, an important asset in a globalised labour market. In a group of international students from all over the world, you have the unique opportunity to encounter foreign cultures and to further develop your intercultural competences.*	
workload calculated in hours of teaching and learning	classroom instruction [hrs] *22.5 hours / 5 workshop days*	assisted self-study [hrs] *10 hours / feedback on the diary*
	independent self-study [hrs] *57.5 hrs*	In total *90 hrs / 3 ECTS*
students' competences at start of module	*Recommended: knowledge of English at conversation level*	
learning outcomes (domain specific competences)	*Participants can...* • *explain the basic concepts and theories of intercultural communication* • *analyse intercultural communication situations* • *describe their own and foreign value systems* • *apply intercultural insights in a work environment*	
learning outcomes (methodological skills)	*Participants can...* • *give presentations in English* • *produce short video clips using mobile phones and open source software*	
learning outcomes (social and personal skills)	*Participants can ...* • *work together with students from other cultures*	

<table>
<tr><td>learning content</td><td colspan="2"><ul><li>Concepts, theories and models of intercultural communication</li><li>Intercultural management, intercultural leadership</li><li>Cultural dimensions in societies</li><li>The value system in cultures and their relationship to human behaviour</li><li>Stereotypes, xenophobia, eurocentrism, ethnopluralism</li></ul></td></tr>
<tr><td>teaching and learning methods</td><td colspan="2">Activity-oriented motivating workshops, interspersed with short lectures</td></tr>
<tr><td>form(s) of assessment</td><td colspan="2"><ul><li>Part A: 50% intercultural video-clip (group work)</li><li>Part B: 25% intercultural diary (individual work / 4 entries)</li><li>Part C: 25% written summary of the reading assignment</li></ul></td></tr>
<tr><td rowspan="2">cognitive level of assessment tasks according to Bloom (specified as a percentage of all tasks)</td><td>reproducing knowledge [%]</td><td>creating [%]
70%</td></tr>
<tr><td>understanding, applying [%]
30%</td><td>evaluating [%]
-</td></tr>
<tr><td>assessment benchmark (individual/personal, social, learning outcome)</td><td colspan="2">Learning outcomes (predefined criteria)</td></tr>
<tr><td>quality of assessment criteria (objectivity, reliability, validity)</td><td colspan="2">-</td></tr>
<tr><td>assessment scale</td><td colspan="2">Pass / fail</td></tr>
<tr><td>required reading</td><td colspan="2"><ul><li>Trompenaars, F., Hampden-Turner, Ch. (2012). Riding the Waves of Culture – Understanding Diversity in Global Business. London: McGraw-Hill.</li><li>Gibson, R. (2010). Intercultural Business Communication. Berlin. Cornelsen.</li></ul></td></tr>
<tr><td>recommended reading</td><td colspan="2"><ul><li>House et al. (2004). Culture, Leadership, and Organization. The CLOBE Study of 62 Societies. Thousand Oaks: Sage.</li></ul></td></tr>
</table>

About the editor

Heinz Bachmann

Heinz Bachmann was a natural science teacher at secondary schools in the Canton of Zurich for 15 years. He also taught in Africa, Latin America and Asia from kindergarten up to secondary school level as well as in high schools and colleges. After completing a second degree in psychology at the University of Zurich, where he also did his PhD, he worked as a teaching advisor and school psychologist. Later, he switched to development cooperation. He currently works as an academic advisor at the Centre for Teaching and Learning in Higher Education at Zurich University of Teacher Education.

In his work, he focuses on:

- higher education teaching,
- learning,
- change management,
- education research,
- intercultural learning and intercultural cooperation.

We welcome feedback about this book to:

heinz.bachmann@hispeed.ch